Winning the Fight Against Breast Cancer:
The Nutritional Approach

Winning the Fight Against Breast Cancer:

The Nutritional Approach

by Carlton Fredericks, Ph. D.

Originally published as Breast Cancer: A Nutritional Approach

Publishers • GROSSET & DUNLAP • New York
A FILMWAYS COMPANY

To April, our beloved daughter.
The thrushes still sing, and we remember,
we remember . . .

Published simultaneously in Canada
Library of Congress catalog card number: 76-50870
ISBN 0-448-12985-X (hardcover)
ISBN 0-448-16527-9 (paperback)
First paperback printing 1979
Printed in the United States of America

Contents

Preface

There are books which must be written, for there are truths which must be shared. Such a book is this, and I write it under that compulsion, ignoring the gratuitous controversy in which it will involve me, for I can no longer excuse the blindness of our health professions to the patent fact that you, the average woman, may help build your resistance to breast and uterine (endometrial) cancer, merely by simple, harmless changes in your eating habits. I simply can no longer abide the realization that the women in my family and among my university students, radio and TV listeners, readers of my books, and patients of the physicians who have acted upon my scientific papers enjoy a nutritional help against a common type of uterine and breast cancer—and *you* don't, because no one has told you that it exists, that it's effective when appropriately applied, and that you can employ it, with immediate dividends, right now.

If our present methods of cancer prevention for women were effective, if, in fact, they really provided prevention, the writing of this book would obviously have been less urgent. But what we call prevention of cancer *isn't*—it is simply early detection, which is a great advance, but it isn't prevention. Consider the implications of a recent magazine article, telling the story of the application of "preventive medicine" in the case of a sixteen-year-old girl in whose family breast cancer has attacked virtually all the women. A professor of preventive medicine at one of the medical schools gave the youngster the full benefits of his art by ordering the tissues of both breasts, though free of cancer, removed, with silicone pads inserted for cosmetic restoration. In a family prone to tooth decay, would it be preventive dentistry to extract all teeth? And what would the professor of preventive medicine recommend in families with a predisposition to leukemia or brain cancer?

Consider: you go for a Pap smear, and it is—we pray—negative. You return for another, at your doctor's chosen interval, and now it's no longer negative, it's precancerous, or early cancer. A great improvement over the older ways, but it is still early recognition dressed in the trappings of prevention. For what will determine your fate primarily will be the kind of cancer which, by this technique, has been recognized early. If it's the type that tends not to migrate, carcinoma in situ, your future is bright. If it's the type that grows and spreads rapidly, the outlook for you, even with early diagnosis, may still be grim. Incidentally, to the fiction that early diagnosis is prevention, the medical statisticians add another: early diagnosis will license the claim that, thanks to modern preventive medicine, you survived longer. Detecting a life-destroying cancer six months earlier, this means, gave you six months longer survival.

Self-examination of the breasts is also called prevention. By the time that the mass is detectable by your untrained fingers, or, for that matter, by the expert touch of your physician's, it may be already five years old, which means that your fate again will depend largely on the nature of the beast that is gnawing at your tissues. The options open to your physician at that moment are limited. The breast can and usually will be removed, with the surgeon choosing between a radical and a modified radical operation. Subsequently, the medical expert will decide whether the nature and extent of the invasion call for postoperative chemotherapy, irradiation, or both. But in how many cases will it later be imperative to remove the other breast, and in how many will the cancer defy the scalpel, irradiation, and drugs, and spread to other parts of the body? Even more pertinent: to what part of all this may the term *prevention* justly be applied? This is not an academic question, for the authorities admit that in the United States alone, at this very moment, there are nearly a quarter of a million women who, unknown to them, harbor breast cancer.

Mammography is an X-ray technique used to try to detect suspicious changes in the breasts before manual examination can identify them. It, too, parades in the robes of prevention. It, too, is simply another aspect of crisis medicine, early detection masquerading as prophylaxis. It carries with it an ironic danger, says the National Cancer Institute, for such frequent X-raying of younger women, below the age of thirty-five, who are less likely to develop the disease, may *cause*, by excessive exposure to irradiation, seventy-five cases of breast cancer for every fifteen it identifies. (As with most subjects in medicine, the experts differ on the degree of risk entailed.)

Thermography, in which the breasts are not irradiated but their heat production recorded on film, is in use as a harmless technique for identifying early cancer. It has its faults—primarily its inability to distinguish between cancer and other diseases which are reflected in altered heat production in affected breast tissues. A variant on this technique is the heat-sensitive bra, but both are open to the same criticisms directed against mammography and against the new laser-beam method of examination: they are ingenious, but they are aspects of our system of crisis medicine—waiting for the small flame, with the hope of preventing the major conflagration. All this is better than nothing, but it is misleading to fail to distinguish between a fire alarm and fireproofing.

Cancer doesn't strike at random or without cause, and usually is the result of more than one insult to the body. As the experts put it, cancer requires more than one "hit." The genes may set the stage, via predisposition, but the genetic tendency is the soil on which the second insult falls and takes root. And that second insult, the factor cavalierly neglected for so many years, may be and frequently is diet, particularly in cancer of the breast and uterus. This book will link at least one third of such cancers with the woman's nutrition—and of all the causes of disease this is surely the most overlooked and the most avoidable. So I said in the context of nutrition versus breast and uterine (endometrial) cancer, more than thirty years ago. So I said of benign uterine fibroid tumors, for which hundreds of thousands of hysterectomies are performed yearly.

The cancer establishment, which in 1976 announced a sudden and vivid interest in nutrition versus cancer, was both hostile to and ignorant of that concept in the preceding decades. In fact, for educating the public in the usefulness of good nutrition to build resistance to some types of cancer, I was, in the 1950s, unofficially but acrimoniously criticized by one of the cancer societies, which described me as offering false hope to the public. I had committed two sins, other than the obvious one of anticipating, twenty years earlier, the establishment's sudden interest in nutrition: (1) I was emphasizing the cancer-causing potential of estrogenic (female) hormone; and (2) I was describing the nutritional chemistry by which good diet bars or minimizes that effect. In short, long before the cancer establishment was ready to accept the theses, I was teaching millions of women how to alter their nutrition to help avoid the type of cancer stimulated by female hormone—the classification in which one third of all breast cancers fall. My medical friends, who were prescribing the hormone for many patients (some of them still are), poured scientific scorn on my thesis, quarreling with it on two cogent bases. Estrogenic hormone, they then insisted, had never been proved to cause cancer. Even if such a link were established, they added, there was no convincing evidence that diet in any way modifies that effect. Well, the evidence existed then, more of it exists now, and this book condenses it. The clues come from nutrition, biochemistry, medicine, endocrinology (glandular chemistry), and epidemiology, or the study of the incidence of disease in population groups. It's all available in any good medical library. And there it is gathering dust, while women die.

Thirty years have passed. Now the medical journals grant that female hormone can cause cancer, though there are still those who argue against the concept. Articles are appearing which stress the dangers of estrogen prescribed by the physician as a contraceptive, in rectifying disturbances of the menstrual cycle, and in treatment of the symptoms of the menopause. But medicine—which jeered initially at a smallpox vaccine, rejected the fever thermometer when it was first invented, and called the electroencephalograph "electronic quackery"—is notoriously slow in accepting new ideas, and still slower in applying them. It will probably take another thirty years before attention is shifted from exterior sources of estrogen, such as the physician prescribes, to interior sources of the hormone, such as the ovaries. An equal number of years will elapse before variation in estrogen production by women is studied from the point of view that high producers of estrogen are giving themselves constant, internally manufactured doses of a cancer-producing hormone. And then finally, a generation later, someone, marshaling the evidence as I did in the years in which I prepared for this book, will happen on two important observations: (1) the fact that the body has protective mechanisms which can disarm estrogen; and (2) that the process is dependent upon the diet.

I don't propose to wait ninety years for this information to surface and find application in preventive nutrition. I don't have the time. You certainly don't. And now you know why this book had to be written.

Introduction

Before the International Academy Metabology, in 1972, I read a paper to a large group of physicians specializing in medical nutrition. It was entitled "Nutritional Management of Estrogen-Dependent Disorders." In it, I explored an unappreciated effectiveness of good nutrition in preventing, controlling, or eliminating disorders in women which are triggered or sustained by excessive activity of female hormone. Included in this list were premenstrual tension, menstrual disturbances, cystic mastitis, uterine fibroid tumors, and, in terms of prevention, breast and uterine cancer. I described the nutritional chemistry which reduces or totally banishes premenstrual tension, water retention, anxiety, depression, hysteria, cramps, backaches, irritability, sensitivity of the breasts, and excessive and prolonged hemorrhaging. I outlined the simple dietary corrections which can minimize or eliminate cystic mastitis, the multiple cysts of the milk producing tubules of the breasts, which can be pre-cancerous. I not only indicted excessive activity of estrogenic (female) hormone as contributing to these disorders in many women, but implicated faulty diet—even in those women physicians consider "well nourished"—in unleashing the mischief-making potential of the hormone. And, long before the mass media told you that estrogens were causing cancer, I labeled the hormone as carcinogenic, and described the nutritional chemistries which can protect women against this deadly effect.

Though some of my medical audience thought the thesis was new, I actually wrote my first publication on the subject in 1945. In a book published in 1950, I urged correction of the diet to protect women against the cancer-producing effects of female hormone—whether prescribed or internally produced. In "Food Facts and Fallacies," a book I wrote in 1958, I repeated the indictment of estrogen as a cancer-causing factor, and again described the biochemistry of nutritional protection against the carcinogenic effect. American women then had not yet heard of the pregnant women dosed with DES (synthetic female hormone) whose daughters were to develop vaginal cancer. The future still held the reports of the tragically increased incidence of cancer in menopausal women treated with the hormone. My thesis for good nutrition to block this estrogen effect was well documented—the evidence went back to the 1930s. So it was that my paper recapitulated the past and made a prophecy for the future when it remarked:

> . . . a rise in Vitamin B Complex intake . . . and in biologically efficient protein will tend to increase the efficiency of hepatic (liver) degradation of estrogen, with frequent and significant improvement in premenstrual tension, dysmenorrhea, cystic mastitis, and other disorders which may be related to hyperestrogenism (excessive levels of estrogenic hormone). . . . this nutritional approach may not only lower estrogen activity to a more physiological level, but may tend to raise the output of estriol. Since estriol–estrogen ratio has been linked with resistance to breast cancer, it may be that the early dividends from improvement of a woman's diet may be less

> significant than the possible long-term reward of increased resistance to estrogen-dependent neoplasms (cancers). . . . any augmentation of estrogen levels—whether of endogenous or exogenous origin (given by nature or by prescription) invites . . . perhaps demands . . . the precautionary measure of correction of the patient's dietary habits.

That paper—published in the Journal of the International Academy Metabology, (Volume IV, Number 1, pages 17–19)—must not, like the evidence preceding it, take years to influence the dietary recommendations made by physicians, and the nutritional habits of American women.

1

The Female Hormone, Crippler and Killer

This is the chemist's shorthand for estrogen—female hormone:

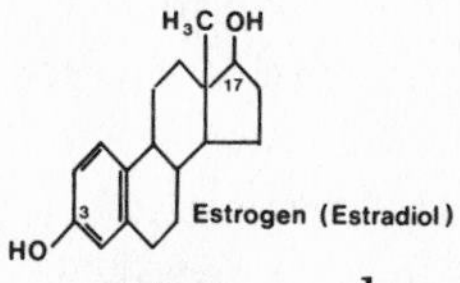

The body breaks down estrogen, degrading it into a much less active, and thereby unthreatening hormone, estriol, the structure of which looks like this:

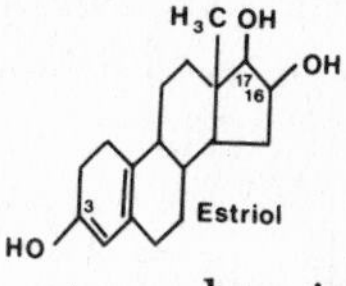

The structural differences between the two chemical diagrams don't seem world-shaking, but they can make the difference between developing breast or uterine cancer or remaining healthy. In converting estrogen into estriol, the body actually turns a carcinogenic (cancer-producing) compound into a harmless chemical, ultimately excreted. Even better than harmless: more estriol and less estrogen means less breast cancer and a reduced tendency to clots and strokes in women overproducing or taking supplementary doses of estrogen, as in the birth control pill. Thus the ratio between the two hormones, as reflected in the urine, can, if favorable, help to block the way to cancer of the sex organs. *This isn't theory:* in population groups where the women tend toward higher estriol and lower estrogen levels, breast cancer is always less frequent.

Two glands convert female hormone into estriol. In one of these, the liver, the process is diet-dependent, and with that chemistry, this book is concerned. And you may judge how important that conversion is by a simple observation: pregnancy has a protective effect against breast cancer for the reason, we believe, that the baby's glands are helping the mother's in breaking down and inactivating estrogen.

If you are blessed with a liver which efficiently converts estrogen into estriol, you effectively pull the fangs of a killer hormone. If your estrogen production is high, as it is in some women, or if you are taking supplements of the hormone in medication or the birth control pill, it means that the tissues of your breasts and uterus are bathed indefinitely in a cancer-producing chemical solution to which they are specifically sensitive and responsive.

The ability of the liver to transform dangerous estrogen into harmless estriol depends implicitly on the adequacy of your diet, that long-neglected factor of resistance to carcinogens (cancer-producing substances). Don't discount that protection. The addition of a rich source of Vitamin B Complex to a diet of hospital scraps sharply reduced the incidence of cancer in animals. The cancer-producing potential of a long-used food dye, butter-yellow, was significantly lowered when the animals were given brewer's yeast. The carcinogenic effect of a chemical which can cause bladder cancer is offset if the urine is rich in Vitamin C.

After nearly thirty years of research, I am convinced that I know which factors in diet are pointedly important in helping the liver to degrade estrogen into its harmless relative, estriol. I have learned, too, that diets we think to be good or even excellent often don't provide ideal amounts of these specific factors, which means that women commonly considered to be well fed often aren't—and the price for their dietary mistakes may start with menstrual disturbances and culminate as breast or uterine cancer.

The evidence supporting that conclusion is drawn from long-term observations of the benefits of improved diet in premenstrual tension, in overprolonged menstruation with excessive hemorrhaging, and in cystic mastitis. Some of the evidence derives from studies of the differences in breast cancer rates in various countries and of what happens when natives of these countries shift to the American diet. Some of it is based on continued dialogues over the last thirty years with medical men whose accumulated observations and collective thinking were generously available to me. Some of the evidence is directly out of the pages of the texts on biochemistry. But you need not be a nutritionist, a biochemist, an epidemiologist, or a physician to understand what this book tells you. It is written for the average woman. And while its prime objective is to help her in building resistance to types of cancer, it has important secondary goals, among which is reducing the impact of the menstrual cycle on a woman's personality, thinking, and functioning.

If the nutritional control of female hormone activity had no effect on resistance to cancer, its actions on the premenstrual week and the menstruation itself would justify adherence to the diet. American women accept, ruefully but passively, the tortures of the premenstrual week and the period as though these are necessary and inescapable prices for the biological birthright of being female and gifted with the ability to bring new life into the world. Actually, the menstruation is a physiological event, not a disease—although it certainly behaves like one. Women suffer premenstrual tension and anxiety, cramps, backache, water retention with weight gain, hysteria, dizziness, fainting, craving for sweets, drawing pains in the thighs, and exquisite sensitivity of the breasts. The impact on the psyche and the cerebral functions is as great: from various authorities, you learn that up to 50 percent of all suicide attempts by women are made in the premenstrual week; that up to 50 percent of all admissions to mental hospitals for women occur in that week; that up to 50 percent of the crimes for which women are jailed are committed in that week. As a person who has taught at many colleges and universities, I can tell you that only a male chauvinist professor would appraise a woman on the basis of her test scores when the examination was given during her premenstrual week, when scores tend to drop at least 15 percent below the woman's actual potential.

You will learn, as you read on, that the efficiency of the estrogen-estriol conversion enters into the dynamics of the menstrual cycle, and that it is also involved in susceptibility to breast cysts—those which appear between ovulation and menstruation, as well as those which take up permanent (and threatening) residence.

Estrogen enters a woman's body in many ways. We tend to focus on the external sources, such as prescribed estrogen, but we sometimes forget that there is estrogen natural to some foods and estrogen added to at least one: beef, the industry having blocked the FDA's ban on the use of diethylstilbestrol (DES) in fattening cattle. Regardless of the sources of the female hormone, your liver must cope with it, converting it into less active compounds, terminating in estriol. On the success of that conversion, your well-being, your life itself, may depend. And for that conversion, your liver requires the help of an excellent diet.

In allowing women to be dosed with estrogen, we may drastically interfere with nature's plans, and you don't do that with impunity. A good example of the exquisite balances nature creates is found in the quail of the California desert, which seem to be endowed with precognition. In seasons when drought will minimize the supply of the seeds on which they feed, they breed less frequently and the quail population is reduced. Only recently was it realized that in drought years, the bushes on which they feed produce extra amounts of estrogen which, in birds as in women, acts as a contraceptive. When the rains are plentiful, the bushes grow more rapidly and profusely, their estrogen output is diluted, and the quail population increases again.

You can't study this minor facet of the chemistry of the sex hormones without developing a healthy respect for the mysteries of nature. Chemically, the differences in the structures of the female and male sex hormones appear slight, but the differences in their actions stagger the mind. Give male hormone to a hen, and she will move inexorably from the bottom toward the top of the pecking order, and may crown that by trying to act like a rooster. Supply excesses of female hormone to the male fetus, and you may dilute his maleness—move him toward femaleness, while causing defects in the development of his genitals. (This actually happened to the boys born to women treated during pregnancy with diethylstilbestrol.)

Merely apply female hormone to the face of a woman, and she may develop cysts of the breast. I learned that initially from experience with a young actress, whose physician had asked me to formulate a high-estrogen (female hormone) cosmetic cream, which he wanted her to try for her problems of very dry skin and premature wrinkling. A few weeks after I delivered the cream to her doctor, the actress called me with a worried question. "My doctor's away," she said, "and I need some advice. Since I've used that cream, I've had cysts in my breasts. I never had them before. When I was on location for a week, and forgot to take the cream with me, the cysts got noticeably smaller, but they grew again when I began using the cream again. Was that coincidence?"

I suggested that she discontinue use of the cream until I could reach her physician, because I had a gut feeling that more than coincidence was involved. Her doctor felt the same way, and he added a comment which became more meaningful after I spent a few months in the library, digging into the literature on estrogen. "There's a significant association," he had remarked, "between chronic cystic disease of the breast and breast cancer." Not until years later did I learn that there are three, mutually exclusive, opinions about *that:*

1. There is no meaningful association between chronic breast cysts and breast cancer.
2. There *is* a strong tendency for chronic cystic mastitis (multiple breast cysts) to be followed by breast cancer.
3. The cancer doesn't *follow* years of breast cysts—it's concealed among them.

The proverbial plague on all their houses, I felt, for I'd often observed that a change in diet, for some women with breast cysts, had been followed by reduction in size, reduction in number, or disappearance of the benign growths. At the time, the thought occurred to me, of course, that in the event that Theory Number 2, above, proves right, such a dietary change might prevent breast cancer.

Because of these thoughts and experiences, I spent years in searching the literature on estrogen, more years in conferring with gynecologists, obstetricians, and endocrinologists, and still more in exchanging thoughts with other nutritionists. But that is leaping through the complex story in quantum jumps. Let's turn to what I learned on my first, long-ago, prolonged visit to the medical library.

I found one authority on cancer stating: "It seems possible that enough estrogens may be elaborated within the bodies of some supposedly normal women to bring about the mammary disturbances out of which cancers come." Some twenty years later I was to learn from Dr. Roger Williams that estrogen production in women varies by a factor of 5, which made me wonder why more attention isn't paid to those with elevated internal production of this cancer-causing hormone. I found surgeons reporting that removing the ovaries of a woman with breast cancer, thereby depriving the growth of hormone stimulation, which was described as a medically accepted procedure, might slow down or even stop the progress of the malignancy. Occasionally, it did more than that: I found a surgeon reporting that such an operation not only caused disappearance of the primary breast cancer, but also resulted in disappearance of an intestinal cancer which started with metastasis from the original malignancy. I read many papers which postulated a link between breast cysts and malignancy, a couple which discussed a relationship between estrogen and breast cysts, but only one or two which even hinted at a possible role of estrogen in breast malignancy. Numerous medical authors attributed to estrogen a decided carcinogenic action, while others rejected that effect. Yet, sandwiched in with these opposing and dogmatic opinions was a flat statement by a cancer specialist, world recognized as an authority on the actions of hormones in the genesis of cancer, that estrogen, given in large doses over a prolonged period, has induced tumors of the breast, cervix, endometrium, pituitary, testicles, and bone marrow in mice, rats, rabbits, hamsters, and dogs. And he said, without reservations, that these animal studies are definitely applicable to women. Since he was head of a department at the National Cancer Institute, a government agency, I thought it passing strange that the medical profession not only ignored his warnings but, if anything, stepped up its prescriptions for estrogen and went on to embrace the birth control pill, containing the hormone, with enthusiasm. Of that pill, this authority said that its estrogen content placed women in a game of Russian roulette, gambling with their lives by pulling the trigger of a revolver with no empty chambers. One is moved to remember, now, that he gave his warning when the Pill had not yet been accused of causing diabetes, hypertension, blood clots, strokes, and other "side reactions" second only to the threat of cancer itself.

In contrast was the attitude of the then Commissioner of the U.S. Food and Drug Administration (FDA), who, when asked about the risk of cancer caused by the estrogen in the newly licensed contraceptive pills, remarked: "We are not justified in barring this drug from the market on the basis of a small statistical risk of cancer." One wondered if he would be quite so complacent about that "slight statistical risk" if he definitely knew that *his* wife might be one of the statistics. It was one of his successors, several times removed, who showed the same myopia concerning the risk of cancer from beef from steers treated with DES, when he warned the American housewife that this estrogenic drug cheapened the cost of production by one cent per pound, so that banning its use would raise the price of meat.* The FDA ultimately did ban it—and the industry promptly reinstated its use, via a court order.

Despite the growing body of evidence indicting estrogen as cancer-producing, physicians wrote increasing numbers of prescriptions for the hormone—and still do so, at the rate of more than $50 million yearly. The majority of these prescriptions were and are addressed to the problems of menopausal women, aimed at relief from the "sweats and flushes" of the change of life, to help keep vaginal tissues from itching and atrophying, and to mitigate osteoporosis, the painful weakening and frequently crippling disease of the bones which incapacitates many postmenopausal women. When challenged concerning the propriety and safety of these long-continued estrogen doses, physicians reminded me that the menopausal woman often has a pronounced deficiency in estrogen, and the prescriptions, which simply

*Such a rise in meat prices would cost the housewife less than $5 per person, per year. A terminal case of cancer can and does frequently cost $100,000—without funeral charges.

restored an accustomed and normal level of the hormone in the body, obviously could cause no harm. Since then, these complacent claims have been negated by a number of retrospective studies which clearly indicate that the administration of estrogen for both menopausal and postmenopausal women strikingly increases the risk of breast and uterine cancer—by a factor from 5 to as much as 14. Even this has not stopped the tide of prescriptions for the hormone, though the manufacturers are now required to warn physicians that the drug must not be prescribed for women with latent cancer. What is latent cancer? Three malignant cells, deep within the breast tissues and indetectable by anything short of studying razor-thin slices of breast tissue under a microscope? And how would the physician select the subjects for such mutilation?

We are, of course, faced again with the realization that much of the testing of drugs is performed on the public, the thalidomide tragedy being an obvious reminder. The public has come to recognize and—if it has not hopelessly succumbed to the worship of the infallibility of the men of medicine—to resent this practice. It has not, however, come to terms with the realization that there are fads in medical prescribing, irrational trends which sometimes inflict gratuitous and great harm. Such a fad, some twenty years ago, resulted in the prescription of synthetic female hormone (DES) for women whose pregnancies were jeopardized by signs of impending spontaneous abortion. Ignoring the fact that precarious pregnancies have been stabilized by harmless nutritional factors, such as wheat germ oil, obstetricians issued a spate of prescriptions for diethylstilbestrol. It rescued many of the pregnancies, but twenty years later, young women exposed to the hormone in the uterus developed precancerous or cancerous changes in vaginal tissues, and some of them died. I've already commented on the price paid by young men who were similarly exposed.

When this synthetic hormone was indicted as the cause

of these disasters, I returned to some of the many physicians with whom I had earlier debated the safety of estrogen, only to find them still unwilling to discard the use of the drug. One of my close medical friends, after I voiced (and documented) my apprehensions in a paper delivered at a medical society meeting, protested: "You can't equate the synthetic female hormone (DES) with the natural. Most of us are prescribing the natural. Stop scaring the profession and the public," he urged. Do you think he surrendered when the later reports indicated that *natural* estrogen is equally carcinogenic? Or switched his female patients from the estrogen-containing contraceptive pills to the IUD?

The battle against the adverse findings on estrogen included, of course, a stout defense by pharmaceutical manufacturers, not surprising with a multimillion-dollar market at stake. Their resistance was implemented not merely by advertisements in the medical journals and by distribution of samples and literature to physicians. It was sometimes subtle. For example, a popular book, written by a physician, vigorously recommended that physicians prescribe estrogen for all women, early enough and in high enough dosage totally to avoid the menopause, with prolonged youthfulness as the promised reward. Nowhere in the book did the reader learn that the author was associated with a foundation deriving part of its funds from grants from the manufacturer of the type of estrogen recommended in the book.

Such conflicts of interest don't mar the performance of the average physician in prescribing estrogen. He is motivated by his concern for his nervous, irritable, anxious, hysterical menopausal women, suffering with their feelings of heat and intense perspiration, their atrophy of vaginal tissues, and their susceptibility to painful weakening of the skeleton. On this basis, he continues to prescribe the hormone. If challenged, he denies or minimizes the risk, or resorts to the doctrine of the "calculated risk." (How does that square with a more ancient philosophy of medicine:

first, do no harm?) It has been soberly pointed out that the medical man does the calculating while the patient takes the risk, but that ultimately, the physician must consider risk versus benefit. If he really does so, there is the strong probability that he will not prescribe estrogen. How does one balance partial (or even total) relief from sweats, flushes, vaginal itching, and weakened bones against the risks of strokes, thrombophlebitis, and cancer? Given the chance at informed consent or rejection, how should, how *would* a woman vote?

There *are* medical problems in which the physician must consider prescribing a dangerous drug, because the question is one of life or death. But this is not so with any of the conditions for which estrogens are prescribed. It must not be thought, either, that physician and patient are without alternative choices, that she must either suffer in silence or else take estrogen, with its benefits and all its risks. There *are* nutritional treatments for the sweats and flushes: Vitamin E, for example, has been known since 1949 to be effective for some women.* Osteoporosis, the weakening of the skeleton, isn't inevitable. It occurs more frequently in women with a lifetime of inadequate calcium intake. Good diet not only helps to avoid it, but harmless nutritional treatments can slow, stop, or even reverse it. (I *know:* for patients of physicians whom I serve as a consultant we've accomplished each of these effects with harmless supplements of calcium orotate and Vitamin D.) No research has been done to find nutrients which will help atrophy and itching of vaginal tissues, nor will it be done: you can't patent a nutrient as you can a drug, which means you can't establish a monopoly and harvest rich profits from such research.

*Question and answer section of the JAMA, 167:1806, 1958: after a complete hysterectomy due to cancer of the ovary, daily doses of 75 units of Vitamin E (in preference to estrogen) were suggested because it "has definite value in diminishing or causing absence of hot flushes."

With all this, the pharmaceutical companies have managed to indoctrinate the physician with the concept that he is locked into the bleak alternatives of the dangers of estrogen or the complaints of tortured patients. With the majority of medical schools unable or unwilling to add nutrition courses to the medical curriculum (and with those courses which are given, devoted to negative nutrition: i.e., what foods to forbid the patient with gallbladder syndrome) the medical man is unlikely to appreciate the effectiveness and safety of the nutritional therapies which he can use to escape the risks of estrogen dosage.

Let us return now to an earlier observation: removal of the ovaries sometimes slows up the progress of breast cancer. The ovaries being the principal sources of estrogen activity in the body, such surgery, of course, deprives the cancer of the stimulation of the hormone. Surgeons learned by experience that about one third of all breast cancers are estrogen-dependent, which means that removal of estrogen from the cancerous tissues will slow or stop the progress of the malignancy. Originally, the operation was performed on a trial-and-error basis, the surgeon hoping that the cancer was of the type which, deprived of estrogen by the surgery, would lose momentum. Not only has experience confirmed that concept of the close relationship between the growth of a common type of breast cancer and the stimulating effect of estrogen, but it has been strengthened by discovery of a technique by which the estrogen-dependent malignancy can positively be identified, for it requires the presence of an estrogen receptor in the tissues. When such a receptor is found, the surgeon need no longer perform the oophorectomy (removal of the ovaries) empirically, with blind hope: he knows that there is a good chance that the induced deficiency of female hormone will slow up such a cancer.

All this led me to seek the answers to several questions of critical importance in the prevention of breast and uterine cancers of the estrogen-dependent type:

1. If there are cancers which respond to female hormone with stimulation of growth, could not such malignancies be *initiated* by high levels of the hormone? Could not the mitosis (reproduction) of the very first cancer cell be accelerated by such levels of estrogen? Might that first cell never have come into being without the constant stimulation of female hormone?

2. If this is so, should we not be as concerned with women who are high estrogen producers as we now are with those who take estrogen?

3. These facts recognized, and direct production of cancer in animals dosed with estrogen also recognized, why must we wait until you have a breast or uterine cancer before we become interested in the reduction of estrogen levels in your body? If you are one of the women who produce five times as much of the hormone as other women do, aren't your estrogen-responsive tissues—breast and uterus—more likely to be overstimulated by this cyclic, rich supply of the hormone? And what if you are a high-level producer of estrogen, and then add more by dosing yourself with a birth-control pill?

4. Will the answers to the preceding questions specifically challenge the practice of many physicians who test women for estrogen levels, and, finding them low, promptly prescribe doses of the hormone?

We do know how to reduce estrogen activity with diet—and good nutrition never drives the body toward the abnormal. We've known how to do this for more than thirty years. That's what this book is all about. Why must we wait to do so until disaster strikes—until the surgeon decides that he must do an oophorectomy as an encore to a mastectomy?

We have known for more than thirty years that women with high estrogen levels and poor diet are more likely to develop breast and uterine cancer. We also have evidence that women with good diets and lower estrogen levels are more likely to escape such cancers.

There is, of course, a valuable clue derived from study of the varying incidence of the disease in population groups here and in other countries. It was by such epidemiological research that we came to realize that the high fiber diet of the Central African protects him against bowel cancer, while shifting to our low-fiber foods makes him as susceptible as we are. He is also markedly resistant to constipation, hemorrhoids, varicose veins, appendicitis, diverticulosis, diverticulitis, and hiatus hernia—which afflict many millions of us. But he does become prey to these disorders when he discards the food selections dictated by the inherited wisdom of the centuries, and shifts to our diets, molded by the uninherited nonwisdom of our food technologists.

Such a truth emerges when we study the incidence of breast cancer in Oriental women who migrate to our country. Japanese women, for instance, are much less prone to breast cancer than American women, but they lose that immunity when, as thousands of them have, they have lived in Hawaii for about ten years. What, other than her diet, does the Japanese woman change when she merges with our culture? We have the answers. We know the nutritional factors needed to protect against breast and endometrial cancer of the estrogen-dependent type. Ironically, the American woman we call *well fed* usually eats a diet deficient in those very nutrients. She pays many prices: disturbances of the premenstrual week and the menstrual, cystic mastitis, uterine fibroid tumors, and a susceptibility to the common type of breast and uterine cancer. My well-educated guess is that six in every ten American women reading this book are actual or potential victims of nutrition which, failing to meet their particular nutritional needs as women, places them in such jeopardy.

2

Good Nutrition Cancels Dangers of Estrogen

Marcia wasn't her real name, but she was a real person whose life (and death) story classically traces the link between a woman's diet and her susceptibility to the breast cancer which destroyed her.

Her troubles crystallized when she had her baby. Pregnancy is a common stress which can upset the delicate balance of the relationships between nutrition and glandular function, although any prolonged, severe pressure on body or mind can and frequently does tilt the scales. She was nearly twenty when she gave birth, after the kind of stormy pregnancy frequent in women whose teen-age and prenatal diets fail to support maximum reproductive efficiency. She returned from the maternity hospital with symptoms of depression, which were dismissed as the "baby blues," but they persisted and turned out to be something more serious, for she drifted away from reality and into outright psychosis. Shock treatment (ECT) was recommended by a psychiatrist who, like so many of these medical practitioners, obviously forgot that his patient not only has a head, but that it is housed in a body. A nutritionist intercepted her before the electro-convulsive treatments could be given, tested her for hypoglycemia (low blood sugar), which can cause depression and psychotic symptoms, and found that she had a severe case of it.

The pathway to low blood sugar is paved with stress inflicted on a poorly nourished body. Excessive consumption of sugar, sensitizing the body into overreaction to this poor food, is a frequent dietary prelude. Contributing factors in Marcia's case included the physiological burden of the pregnancy, superimposed on the toll for years of malnutrition; allergies, of which she had several severe ones; and excessive use of caffeine—she consumed large amounts of heavily sweetened coffee and great quantities of cola drinks, which are also laden with sugar and caffeine. The bankruptcy of her diet was clearly reflected in other symptoms, ignored by her psychiatrist, including many stretch marks, many white spots on her nails, nausea which interfered with eating for nearly seven months during her pregnancy, and a sudden inability to remember her dreams—an often unnoticed effect of a severe deficiency in a B vitamin.

As the nutritionist anticipated, Marcia's psychotic behavior disappeared when she was persuaded to eat the type of diet which sustains normal levels of blood sugar. Such a diet is low in sugar, because hypoglycemics overreact to it and burn it too fast (the more they eat of it, the less they have); it is high in protein, which supplies lasting energy; and it is served in frequent small meals. Accompanying the diet were supplements of vitamins, minerals, and a natural source of the Vitamin B Complex. *Consistent* use of such a diet plan is essential if patients with low blood sugar are to rehabilitate liver and adrenal functions.

Marcia was largely unaware of her recovery from psychosis, having been unaware of her departures from reality, but she did comment, as she remained on the nutritional regime, on the improvement in her premenstrual symptoms, with particular reference to the permanent disappearance of the breast cysts which had been, she said, her unfailing warning that her period was approaching. The nutritionist warned her that she must stay with her new diet, for tissues which have been insulted nutritionally remember it. He told her that the cysts were another of the prices for the precarious diet which had been the prelude to the hypoglycemia, and that they would be a portent of more serious troubles to come, if she didn't commit herself to consistent good nutrition. However, she was deaf to his description of the relationships among food, liver function, and estrogenic hormone activities, and so, a few years later, she had to consult a gynecologist, complaining that her menstruals had lengthened until, as she put it, one period ran into the next. He found uterine fibroid tumors, and, after lesser methods had failed to stop the bleeding, referred her for surgery. The uterus was removed, but the ovaries left intact, to avoid a surgical menopause (translation: to keep estrogen levels up).

Still refusing to accept the link between her troubles and her diet, Marcia gradually returned to her sweet tooth and menu pattern of one meal a day. Not only did the hypoglycemia return, but now she showed signs of a latent diabetes, to which low blood sugar is often the prelude. The transient breast cysts, which formerly had appeared after ovulation and disappeared with the menstrual, became permanent visitors, which is to say that she had developed cystic mastitis. She refused surgery for these—were they not benign? But the benign cysts were followed by cancer of her right breast, which now involved her in a mastectomy, followed by chemotherapy and irradiation.

Though the surgeon said he was sure he had "gotten it all," the disease process continued. Lymph nodes became involved, and then cancer appeared in the other breast. She underwent a second mastectomy, followed again by irradiation and chemotherapy. Three years later, cancer killed her. It is Marcia's story, but you know that it is the story of many millions of women.

Look now at the nutritional chemistry which, applied early enough, might have spared this young woman:

As we have neglected the patent fact that estrogen plays a role in cancer of the sex organs in women, so have we closed our eyes to the direct relationship between the diet and many other estrogen-dependent disorders. Yet we have seen stoppage of menstruation in starvation, in obesity (alimentary castration is the old name for that association), in women with anorexia nervosa (psychogenic loss of appetite), and in those who have abused themselves with long-continued drastic reducing diets.

Before the turn of the century, it was fashionable for women to be glamorously anemic, particularly around puberty. That type of anemia was called "chorosis" because their complexions had a greenish tint. That is not important to you, but what *is* important is the fact that with the anemia came abnormal uterine bleeding in the absence of usual physical causes, such as uterine fibroid tumors. When female alcoholics develop cirrhosis of the liver, physicians anticipate excessive uterine bleeding as one of the penalties for substitution of liquor for food, a dietary pattern which interferes with the women's ability to inactivate female hormone. (In this context, remember that estrogen can cause bleeding even in seventy-year-old women!) In pellagra, a deficiency disease stemming from inadequate intake of protein and Vitamin B Complex, excessive menstrual hemorrhaging is a frequent symptom.

From hindsight, we now know that the common denominator in all these pathways to menstrual disturbances and hemorrhaging is excessive estrogen activity as a by-product of disturbed liver function. Which doesn't deter the latter-day endocrinologist (gland specialist) from dosing women with estrogens and other hormones without inquiry into their eating habits. Not only is the specialist innocent of training in nutrition, which medical school curricula largely ignore, but how do we convince him that the patient he considers "well nourished" *isn't*—or she wouldn't have had the symptoms which made her visit him?

Unfortunately, the belief has held for decades that the concomitance of dietary deficiency and glandular disturbances in both men and women is coincidental. Even when the evidence was clear that lessons learned from animal research were directly applicable to human beings of both sexes, improper conclusions were drawn. A classic example of this was the atrophy of the testicles found in veterans of World War II who, on their return from Army service, were complaining of infertility. Similar testicular atrophy was known to occur in rats deprived of Vitamin E; deficiency of Vitamin E was characteristic of the battle rations on which many of these soldiers had lived for months; but doses of Vitamin E didn't reverse the condition, which, of course, led to the facile conclusion that lack of this vitamin may cause atrophy of the testicles in rats, but has nothing to do with the condition in man. No one paused to realize that the atrophy in rats is *also* not reversed by the vitamin when the degeneration of the testicles passes the point of no return.

In 1929, when the first of the female hormones, theelin, was isolated, it shortly became apparent that this factor is destroyed somewhere in the body. A few years later came the realization that the liver, charged with the responsibility for detoxifying many chemical hazards in the body's internal environment, might be the organ which inactivates the hormone. This was first demonstrated in the test tube, where it was observed that liver tissue will destroy more than 80 percent of added estrogen. By observing the sexual receptivity of female rats, which is triggered by female hormone, it was then proved that the flow of estrogen through the liver could be turned on or off by feeding or withholding the B vitamins in the diet. It was shown that the impairment of the estrogen-inactivating mechanism of the liver was on a purely biochemical, rather than physical basis, meaning that a malnourished liver, however normal in appearance, would fail to break down estrogen, and a liver grossly degenerated, showing extensive destruction of cells and infiltration with fat, was nonetheless effective in degrading estrogen *if* the diet was adequate. It became possible to pinpoint the nutritional factors critical to support of this liver function. They proved to be in the Vitamin B Complex, a group of vitamins so called because they tend to occur together in foods. This degradation of estrogen was demonstrably inefficient with a diet low in B vitamins and highly effective in the presence of an adequate supply of these nutrients, provided by a good diet.

All the early research, though, was performed with laboratory rats. Not only were its implications for women not considered—because estrogen then had not been linked with cancer—but the thesis, even when involving only laboratory animals, became the focal point of the disagreements which surround any scientific advance. It wasn't deficiency in the B vitamins that interfered with the role of the liver in impeding estrogen activity, said the critics. It was loss of appetite and consequent reduction of gross food intake, which has long been known to be an effect of deficiency in the B vitamins. The criticism proved invalid, but it took years of research to settle the argument, and to demonstrate that vitamin deficiency itself, rather than inadequate food intake, was the critical factor; but all this was still applied in terms of the nutrition and the glandular chemistry of rats alone.

When the principle was finally applied clinically, in the physicians' management of estrogen-dependent disorders in women, it became obvious that there is a liver-centered mechanism in both rats and humans that is specific for inactivation of estrogen as well as clearly diet-dependent, though the liver of the animal depends for that function on different vitamins of the B Complex. Protein also proved to be a critical nutrient to support this liver function, for the vitamins were ineffective if the diet contained too little of such foods as meat, fish, fowl, eggs, or dairy products. Much later, it was found that "well-fed" women with estrogen-dependent disorders, ranging from premenstrual tension and prolonged menstruation to excessive hemorrhaging and cystic mastitis, lost their symptoms when more generously supplied with the Vitamin B Complex and protein, which, of course, begs the question: is our nutritional standard for a "well-fed" woman too low? The point involved is illustrated in the rat's requirement for Vitamin A, for the daily intake which will protect the animal's eyes is strikingly less than the potency needed for reproductive efficiency. What, then, are the criteria by which we label a rat as "well fed"? Similarly, the intake of Vitamin B Complex that helps to protect a woman against pellagra or beriberi may be far below what she needs to bar the effects of excessive estrogen activity.

Between the 1930s and 1940s, evidence was accumulated (and ignored) which related high levels of estrogen to abnormal uterine bleeding, chronic cystic mastitis, endometriosis, uterine fibroids, excessive tendency to blood clotting, and breast and uterine cancer. It seemed logical then to blame such elevated levels of female hormone on overactivity of the ovaries, just as it seems logical to blame excessive intake of cholesterol for high blood levels. But high blood cholesterol may result, instead, from inadequate *excretion* of the factor, induced by Vitamin C deficiency; and high estrogen levels may easily reflect inadequate inactivation of the hormone, because of liver dysfunction based on nutritional deficiency, rather than elevated production of estrogen.

It must be remembered—few do remember—that the body must cope with estrogen from many sources, of which the ovaries are just one. Women produce male as well as female hormone, and some women manage to convert male hormone into estrogen, thereby augmenting the body burden of female hormone. There is natural estrogen in foods—in whole grains, for instance. There are drugs which potentiate estrogen effects—one of the common tranquilizers is an example. There are nutrients which have at least a weak estrogen effect—the bioflavonoids, for example. There are at least two vitamins which increase the estrogen effect, as well as two which lessen it. There are sometimes traces in meat of the synthetic hormone, accruing from its insane use in fattening animals. And there is the tide of estrogen prescribed by physicians, directly or as a component of birth-control pills. This is a portrait of potential disaster: acquire enough estrogen from such sources, and disarm the body's control mechanism by eating as carelessly as millions of American women do, and you can—as Marcia did—commit a form of attenuated nutritional suicide, a legal kind of self-destruction.

The details of how to shape your nutrition to raise your resistance to breast and uterine cancer are fully discussed in Chapter 6, but for the moment, accept this statement: a majority of American women commit at least six dietary errors which dilute their resistance to estrogen-dependent disorders, ranging from menstrual disturbances to such cancers. And *that* explains why the Japanese woman loses her resistance to breast cancer when she migrates to our country, and shares your nutritional habits—and mistakes. The process of Americanizing her, in that invidious sense, takes only ten years. You have a head start, which, if this book reaches its mark, you will promptly cancel.

Deficiency in the B vitamins is the beginning of a vicious cycle, for the estrogen–Vitamin B Complex equation operates both forward and backward. Not only does lack of the B vitamins raise estrogen levels by interfering with inactivation, but high levels of the hormone will cause symptoms of Vitamin B Complex deficiency. This has been observed in women who take estrogen-based birth control pills, which are now known to cause deficiencies in Vitamin B_6, Vitamin B_{12}, and folic acid.

I have seen administration of estrogen worsen the effects of nutritional inadequacy. I have watched symptoms of such dietary deficiencies intensify as women enter the high-estrogen phase of the menstrual cycle. This also happens during the latter part of pregnancy, when there is a pronounced rise in the body burden of female hormone. This is directly related to the menstrual disturbances which so often follow pregnancy: increase in the amount and duration of hemorrhaging, intensified premenstrual tension, and the appearance or the aggravation of cystic mastitis. It is also related to uterine involution, or the organs' return to normal after childbirth. This process, when estrogen levels are abnormally high, is sometimes much slower or less complete than it should be.

That the problem is directly related to the diet has been clearly demonstrated in a controlled study of two large groups of pregnant women, 107 of whom were maintained on usual pregnancy diets. The other group, 76 women, were given such diets, but also took generous supplements of Vitamin B Complex. In the unsupplemented group, 6 patients had poor involution of the uterus, in 23 it was fair, it was good in 78, and it was excellent in none. In the group receiving the vitamin supplement, none had poor involution, in 3 it was fair, in 56 it was good, and in 17 it was excellent. This means that only 73 percent of the group on the average pregnancy diet had satisfactory involution of the uterus, as against 96 percent of those receiving the bonus of Vitamin B Complex. I emphasize that a majority of medical men and most registered dietitians would have balked at recommending use of the vitamin supplement, for the good reason that in their indoctrination (*not* education) they are taught that American diet is superb and that anyone who differs is undoubtedly the proprietor of a vitamin company.

In similarly refreshing contrast was the experience of female students at Fairleigh Dickinson University, where I conducted long-term research on the influence of improved diet on the menstrual cycle. The nutrition of the test subjects was bettered with an increase in Vitamin B Complex intake, whether from supplements, special-purpose foods such as dried liver or yeast, better choices of food, or a combination of these, or from reduced intake of sugar—which, even as the sole change in the diet, will often shorten menstruation and reduce premenstrual tension—and adjustment of protein intake, where necessary. Let me emphasize again that the women who participated in this research would initially have been labeled as healthy and well fed, and thereby in no need of improvements in their diets.

To relieve the minds of those who worship at the shrine of the blind experiment, a research method intended to eliminate the influence of the power of suggestion, let me also note that the test and control groups did not know, until the results were tabulated, that we were solely interested in control of estrogen activity, via improved nutrition, and in its impact on premenstrual tension and the menstrual cycle. Many of these 300 young women considered their menstruation normal if the bleeding lasted five or six days, but long before the end of the experiment a majority of them reported that their periods had shortened to three or four days, the effect requiring a few months to eventuate. This research brings up two interesting possibilities: (1) with the menstrual cycle, as with so many other phenomena, we tend to interpret the average as the norm (i.e., it's normal to have loose teeth if you're over thirty-five, because 80 percent of all Americans in that age bracket do); and (2) it's quite possible that a five-day period isn't normal, but average, and is, furthermore, an average penalty for a diet considered normal because it's average. Remembering again that all the women in this experiment initially considered themselves well fed, healthy, and normal and came to realize that they weren't, may I ask you, the reader, what is the standard by which we should judge a woman as being well fed—and what makes you think that you meet it?

Shortening of the period was but one of the dividends accruing from simple, easily achieved changes in diet. Women who are resigned to a prolonged and painful menstruation are often also reconciled to premenstrual tension, with its anxiety, hysteria (the word comes from the Greek term for uterus), nervousness, fatigability, irritability, insomnia, tenderness and cysts of the breasts, drawing pains in the thighs, backache, water retention with weight gain, fuzziness of thinking, difficulty in concentrating, craving for sweets, fainting spells, cramps, and dizziness. These average preludes to an impending, prolonged menstruation disappeared or were significantly reduced in intensity in a large majority of these college women. Typically, they commented on the fact that after a month or two of improved diet, the menstruation appeared without the usual preliminary warning symptoms. A typical remark was: "I used to know my period was coming because I climbed walls. Now I know it's coming when it arrives." The most enthusiastic response came from a girl who for ten years had suffered from chronic cystic mastitis, so painful that she routinely slept with a bra on, to minimize the pain she suffered if in sleep she placed pressure on her breasts. She said: "As a man, you can't imagine what it means to me to be able to turn over in bed without being awakened by pain. My doctor," she added, "had been bugging me to have the cysts removed, and he still doesn't believe what has happened." (Initial observations on diet versus estrogen versus breast cysts were published by a physician in 1931, nearly a half century ago. This is another example of the aggravated cultural lag in nutrition, which can no longer be condoned.)

The experiment at the university ended nearly twenty years ago, and I resisted the temptation then to tell this woman that these were early dividends from a nutritional process of estrogen control which, in the long term, might mean increased resistance to types of estrogen-dependent cancer in women. I could have been less conservative, for even then there was significant evidence, gathered in a study by a physician at McGill Medical School, to back my optimism. That research involved two groups of women, equated for age distribution, one group suffering with uterine cancer, the other essentially healthy. A very large majority of the cancer patients displayed high levels of estrogen, low intake of Vitamin B, and low blood levels of the vitamin. By coincidence, exactly the same percentage (94.5 percent) of the healthy patients had high intake of Vitamin B, high blood levels, and normal or low levels of estrogen. The study involved only Vitamin B_1, but the intake of that vitamin may be used as a rough index of the intake of other vitamins of the B Complex, since they tend to occur together in foods. The results, of course, confirm both of the theses of this book: inadequate intake of Vitamin B Complex unleashes undesirably high levels of active estrogen, which in turn is meaningfully associated with uterine cancer.

The point can't be overemphasized. We have evidence that administration of estrogen greatly increases the risk of cancer in women. We know that estrogen ingested by a pregnant woman may (and has been shown to) increase the risk of cancer for her unborn baby daughter twenty years later. Given doses of the hormone, or high body levels because of poor diet, for what good reason would the chemistry of carcinogenesis fail to operate?

Though the women's liberation movement has reemphasized the fact that women are not men, it is interesting that the relationship between diet and estrogen activity is displayed in the male sex, too. In male alcoholics, an early symptom of the liver disease to which they are prone is the disappearance of the hair on the chest, frequently accompanied by enlargement of the breasts. These are, of course, the feminization effects of elevated estrogen levels. In men dosed with estrogen—in the naive belief that it is this hormone alone which protects women against the male susceptibility to heart attacks—cancer of the breast, a site vanishingly rare in men, has resulted. It is a phenomenon which should arrest the attention of every woman whose premenstrual rise in estrogen activity stimulates her breasts, increasing their size and sensitivity, causing pain or inducing the growth of cysts.

It is a fact that much of what we first learned about the body's management of estrogen derived from research with men, rather than with women. Ordinarily, the male has a dominance of testosterone (male hormone) and is untroubled by excessive estrogen activity. But there have been circumstances where the ratio of the two hormones was abnormally changed, with striking dilution of masculine characteristics as a result. Such phenomena occurred in prison camps during World War II, when American medical men, themselves prisoners, observed that the starvation diet was obviously shifting male prisoners toward the feminine, with enlargement of the breasts, less frequent need for shaving, and total loss of the sex drive. These symptoms, paradoxically, increased when food packages provided brief periods of better nutrition, which puzzled the Army physicians. If starvation was causing a rise in female hormone activity, why would a short period of better diet aggravate the symptoms?

The riddle was revived when the prisoners were repatriated and treated with high-calorie, nutritious diets, generously supplemented with vitamin concentrates. In the first week or two, the shift toward the feminine became more pronounced, and then slowly disappeared. From the vantage point of hindsight, the riddle is easily solved. The malnourished liver often requires months of proper nutrition before it fully responds. An improved diet, though, will *promptly* stimulate hormone production. So it was that in the first week or two, the symptoms of feminization intensified, for estrogen production was rising and the restraining influence of the liver was not yet operative.

Exactly the same responses are observed in some women when they improve their nutrition. In the first menstruation following the change in diet, they may experience somewhat intensified disturbances premenstrually and during the period. This reflects a transient rise in estrogen production, stimulated by better nutrition, exactly as it appeared in the prisoners. Continuing with the better diet, the women enjoy the delayed benefits of improved liver function by the second menstruation, when improvement is often so striking that those who experience it are at first startled, and then indignant because no one had ever hinted that there is a relationship between menstruation and nutrition.

In the light of what you have read, you might now reread the history of Marcia. She was a victim of a lifetime of faulty dietary habits which impaired liver function. Part of the price was her hypoglycemia, which, remember, was in part triggered by excessive sugar intake. (There is a .64 correlation between sugar consumption and breast cancer, meaning that 64 times in every 100, you will find a higher incidence of the disease associated with higher intake of sweets.) Part was her premenstrual disturbances, and another was the cystic mastitis. The breast cancer wasn't a dispensation from an indifferent providence. It, too, emerged from the same process. Of what use are surgery, irradiation, and chemotherapy for cancer of a breast when the process which caused the malignancy has been operating for the woman's adult life-span—and is still assaulting the other breast? When the ovaries, so thoughtfully spared in Marcia's hysterectomy (to avoid surgical menopause), are still generously producing estrogen which the liver, crippled by a lifetime of indifferent nutrition, can't suppress?

And now for a warning to the reader: the next chapter covers highly technical subjects. Every one of them is related to our central thesis: how a woman can adjust her nutrition to prevent a type of cancer common in women. Reading it will call for patience and thought—but, at that, less travail than waiting for the results of a Pap test, mammography, or X-ray diagnosis!

3

Warning Voices, Deaf Ears, and a Toll of Disasters

> At current rates, some 89,000 women will develop breast cancer this year in the United States alone. It is expected that, of these, 47 percent will have axillary metastases. [Editor's note: they are well on the way to serious trouble.] These 42,000 women cannot all go to the approximately 200 university hospitals and research institutions in the country. As many as can should, so the absolute therapy may some day be found. But emotional, economic, and logistic considerations preclude this option for the majority.

The preceding statement, by Dr. James F. Holland, an oncologist (cancer specialist) at Mt. Sinai School of Medicine in New York, is a representative sample of the American philosophy of crisis medicine: we must study the patients with this disease so that we may arrive at the proper combination of toxic drugs which will cure without fail—though obviously not in time for the 32,000 women whose breast cancers, in this single year, will kill them.

In contrast, consider a statement made to me by a great medical biochemist–nutritionist, Dr. I. N. Kugelmass, editor of some 500 titles in the *Living Chemistry* series of medical monographs:

> In carcinogenesis, four fifths of our ambient mutation rate is environmental in origin and could be eliminated by environmental hygiene relating to food, additives, drugs, air pollutants, water, and certain virus infections. About 10 percent of that quota can be attributed to the natural radiation background, which is unavoidable,* and an equal proportion to artificial radiation. The major source of artificial radiation today is diagnostic X rays.

Apart from the expert's implicit condemnation of mammography as a possible cause of breast cancer, that paragraph lists at least three sources of cancer about which *you* can do something: food and food additives, water, and drugs. Of these, more later.

Now consider a note from a layman, a representative sample of hundreds of thousands I've received in the past thirty years:

> My doctor brusquely brushed me off when I quoted your statement that good diet and proper use of vitamin/mineral supplements might prevent or treat cystic mastitis, which I have had for several years; and also, when I quoted you as saying that it might help to prevent breast cancer. He said that the claims made for nutrition are excessive and unverified, and he denied that estrogen—which he prescribes—can cause cancer. Why are so many physicians negative about nutrition?

Before I respond to the question, just by way of contrast, let me quote a remark in a letter from one of my readers: "Dear Doctor Fredericks: I follow *all* your advice since you showed me how to clear myself of cystic mastitis—and keep

*There is a technique in nutrition which may help to raise resistance to the effects of radiation, both artificial and natural.—C.F.

it so, for five years." Such letters, of course, constitute anecdotal evidence, to which the scientific establishment is markedly allergic, on the obvious grounds that my reader's confidence in me was the basis on which the cysts disappeared, making the power of suggestion an antidote for estrogen effects on the cystic breast.

The following, however, is a comment from an observer distinctly not susceptible to suggestion: the head of the department of gynecology at a major hospital. He called me at the request of a patient, a young woman who was familiar with my research in nutrition versus cystic mastitis and uterine fibroid tumors. The patient's condition was precarious; she had been hemorrhaging, because of the tumors, for several months before she visited the physician, and, as he put it, she was bled so white that he seriously considered a blood transfusion. The diagnosis, he said, was firm: she definitely had uterine fibroid tumors, to confirm which they had performed a histogram, a type of X-ray examination which is used to overcome the difficulties of using ordinary irradiation techniques to explore soft tissues. She also had a severe cystic mastitis. Usual gynecological therapies had not stopped the hemorrhaging, and he was considering a hysterectomy, to which the patient objected, both because she was not yet thirty and because she wanted at some future date to have children.

"If you have anything in nutrition which might diminish this bleeding," the doctor said, "and possibly help the cystic mastitis, I'll entertain using it." He allotted me an optimistic two weeks in which to accomplish this small miracle, as he put it. As it eventuated, the small miracle required some sixteen days, when the hemorrhaging was markedly reduced. A month later, it had stopped and the patient and doctor both noticed a reduction in the size of the breast cysts. I asked for a follow-up report, which I received about six months later. The physician called, making a contradictory remark:

"Mrs. F. is doing very well. The cystic mastitis is no longer present, the hemorrhaging has not returned, and the examination is essentially negative."

Since "essentially negative" means what it says, I asked: "What about the uterine fibroids?"

Said the physician "They're gone—but uterine fibroids don't disappear."

I made the obvious reply: "Did she have them?" He said she definitely did: "The histogram confirmed *that.*" To which I responded: "Either she had them, and they disappeared, or she didn't have them to begin with. Your position, doctor, is untenable." He laughed, and we ended the conversation.

That patient is now fifty years old. She never had the hysterectomy, the uterine fibroids and the cystic mastitis never again troubled her. No medications were used—just a diet low in refined sugar and processed carbohydrates, supplemented with a properly formulated Vitamin B Complex concentrate, and added brewer's yeast and desiccated liver. And I suspect that the good physician, if ever he does think about this patient, still has reservations about the application of nutrition in gynecological problems. I should add that this response—the disappearance of uterine fibroid tumors—though it is mentioned in European medical articles on nutrition, is rare in my experience, even though in cystic mastitis it is quite frequent. I suspect that it is much easier to prevent or retard the growth of uterine fibroids with good nutrition than it is to treat them.

Coming back to the question concerning the negative attitude of many physicians toward nutrition, a partial answer is found in an editorial in the November 29, 1976, *Journal of the American Medical Association* (JAMA). It tells the story of the responses of 60 medical schools to detailed questions concerning the amount of instruction in nutrition which their students receive. Sixteen schools didn't respond. Seven stated they offer no instruction in nutrition, though one must assume that their graduates will nonetheless dispense diets, nutritional guidance, and negative thoughts about nutrition to their patients. Two schools offer 1 hour of nutrition education—in 4,000 hours of medical courses. Eleven offer 2 to 10 hours; nine give 11 to 19 hours; three offer 20 to 40 hours, and only one has a complete department of nutrition. For purposes of comparison, let me note that I have taught—and still do teach—basic and advanced nutrition courses at a number of colleges and universities. Those courses require 60 hours of classroom study, and certainly can't be described as qualifying students to assume a position of authority, or to dispense nutritional advice and counsel to the public.

The remainder of the medical schools responded that the subject was "touched on" in other courses, or that there was an elective seminar given, or that it was part of public health instruction, or that the students could, if they chose, "work with the dietitian." Vis-à-vis the last resource: in giving lectures and seminars to hundreds of dietitians, including many registered with the American Dietetic Association, for some twenty-five years, I have not yet encountered one who was aware that there is a role of nutrition in the metabolism of estrogen. In fact, a group of registered dietitians, associated with the Chicago Nutrition Association, which condemns any author with whom it disagrees, assured one of my publishers that there is no documentation for my statement that the degradation of estrogen is clearly diet dependent. I supplied the documentation, which included a statement by the AMA, but the Chicago group was not about to let ugly facts interfere with their theories.

To conclude the review of the *JAMA* editorial: it noted that a similar survey was made of departments of animal husbandry in various colleges. Thirty were queried, and all replied, and all thirty declared that they teach animal nutrition in many courses. (If you want to be well fed, be a thoroughbred horse or a pedigreed dog. I've learned more nutrition from veterinarian journals than from those in medicine!)

Before the physician can accept the application of nutrition in pulling the fangs of estrogenic hormones, he must overcome roadblocks in his thinking, the first of which is well said in the old New England axiom: we tend to be down on what we're not up on. But lack of training in the chemistry of foods, so graphically portrayed in the *JAMA* editorial, isn't the only explanation. The body requires some fifty nutrients, which operate in an intricate system in interdependence and co- and counterplay. This means that a nutritional disturbance in the body must reflect such interactions and, in turn, that nutritional treatment, whether therapeutic or preventive, must call for a complex prescription of many nutrients. But the physician is taught that complex prescriptions are irrational, for it becomes impossible to determine which ingredient did what. He therefore has a built-in resistance to the type of treatment used by medical nutritionists, since a prescription for more than one or two vitamins, minerals, or amino acids directly collides with his training, and it doesn't occur to him that a rule which operates well with toxic drugs is not appropriately applied to harmless nutrients, which, rationally, should not be prescribed singly.

As for his reluctance to accept estrogen—whether prescribed or internally produced—as carcinogenic, you must remember that only very recently have environmental factors been recognized as the causes of four cases of cancer in every five. This calls for a shift in the thinking on the part of medical men, who have leaned heavily on genetics to explain malignancy. And major shifts in medical philosophy and practice are notoriously pedestrian. Consider that the doctor who first proposed to treat cancer with X-ray irradiation was initially persecuted by his peers.

It is also possible that at the deepest level of the physician's thinking is an understandable reluctance to accept culpability in having prescribed a hormone which is a killer. Add to this a wariness concerning nutrition in medical practice, and you will have to search for medical men willing to employ corrected diet as a means of preventing types of cancer common in women.

There are many exceptions, of course. At least five medical societies in the United States are devoted to holistic, preventive medicine, and therefore their members are vitally interested in nutrition. In contrast to the philosophies portrayed earlier in this chapter, consider this communication which I received from an internist, a graduate of Johns Hopkins:

> I learned from your paper, "Nutritional Management of Estrogen-Dependent Disorders," how to protect my patients when I find it necessary to prescribe estrogens. I carefully supervise their diets, with appropriate food supplements, following faithfully the method you described at the convention of the International Academy Metabology.

There are now hundreds of physicians who read that paper or heard it discussed, and understand the use of the chemistry of nutrition in blocking the evil effects of female hormone; but hundreds of thousands remain to be educated. Since the diet of the well person is usually self-selected, I've chosen now—after years of effort with the profession—to speed the process by turning to the American woman, knowing that the grass roots method is perhaps the most effective way of shortening the cultural lag characteristic inherent in the field of medicine.

It was in late 1975 that I became aware that a group at the School of Public Health at Harvard University were studying skin-fold thickness of Oriental women living in Hawaii and in their native lands. They were, of course, aware of the Oriental woman's high resistance to breast cancer and how it ebbs when she settles in our culture, and were obviously trying to identify a relationship between the amount of fat in the body and susceptibility to breast malignancies—their supposition being, I surmise, that on the American diet there is a tendency for the composition of the body to change, as more fat is consumed.

I wrote to the Harvard group, suggesting that it would be profitable to divert attention from skin-fold thickness to the direct role of diet in impeding estrogen. I anticipated the subsequent interest displayed by the Harvard researchers, knowing that at least one physician in the group has long been concerned with the "estrogen profile" of women as one of the determinants of the breast-cancer risk. Dr. Philip Cole, of Harvard, has published important papers on the estriol quotients of different populations, which exhibit different rates of incidence of cancer. His preliminary findings strongly link high levels of degraded estrogen (estriol) with elevated resistance to breast malignancy. As I noted earlier, this is markedly exhibited in Oriental women, who, until they live in Hawaii for ten years, have only 20 percent of the rate of breast cancer obtaining in American and Canadian women. But nowhere in the Harvard papers is reflected an awareness of a *specific* action of the diet in determining the estrogen-estriol ratio, however suggestive may be the rise in incidence of breast cancer in Oriental women who discard soybean curd and raw fish in exchange for hamburgers, doughnuts, pizza, soda pop, white bread, and one hundred pounds or more of sugar yearly.

The research with skin-fold thickness relates to an ancient observation that obese women have more breast cancers than those of normal weight.* They also display other evidences of glandular disturbances, ranging from skipping of menstruation to excessive hemorrhaging. Animal studies corroborate, for overweight mice are known to develop

*This is not attributed to obesity, in and of itself, but to the fact that overweight people are products of a bad diet, and reflect its deficiencies.

more mammary cancers, and fewer appear when the animals are on calorie-restricted diets. Obesity is also linked with excessive estrogen activity based on dietary inadequacy, which means that fat women are malnourished women, with particular emphasis on inadequate intake of the Vitamin B Complex. The acute importance of that observation is emphasized by a physician who observed regressions in breast cancers in animals, following administration of a rich source of the B Complex vitamins. The lesson you have just learned is pointed: it's better to be slim and well nourished, if you don't want breast cancer.

Earlier, I partially quoted some of the researchers who have demonstrated that estrogen is carcinogenic, capable of initiating and stimulating cancer. I should like now to retrace those statements in full, identifying the authorities who made them, which will help you to realize that this book is based on concrete evidence, rather than my personal conviction that there are links among estrogen, diet, and uterine and breast cancer.

Dr. Roy Hertz, formerly head of endocrinology (gland function) at the National Cancer Institute, a government agency, was regarded worldwide as an authority on the roles of hormones in cancer. His statements on estrogen included this one, which was quoted verbatim in a publication of the American Cancer Society, *eight years ago:*

> For many years, the profound effects of hormones on cancer of the breast and female genital tract have been known. . . . we know that estrogens, when given in large doses over a prolonged period, will induce tumors of the breast, cervix, endometrium, pituitary, testicles, kidney, and bone marrow in mice, rats, rabbits, hamsters, and dogs. *These studies are applicable to man.* [Emphasis added.]

This was said eight years ago. In those eight years, American physicians prescribed some $400,000,000 worth of estrogen, not counting that supplied in many of the birth control pills.

It was the eminent Dr. Ludwig Kast, in a paper delivered at the Graduate Fortnight of the New York Academy of Medicine, who shifted attention from exogenous (administered) estrogen to internally manufactured, when he remarked: "It seems possible that enough estrogens may be elaborated within the bodies of some supposedly normal women to bring about the mammary disturbances out of which cancers come." Was anyone listening?

Dr. S. G. Taylor, writing in the *Journal of Surgery, Gynecology, and Obstetrics,* squarely indicted female hormone as being linked to breast cancer, when he wrote: "It is well known that about one third of breast cancer in premenopausal women is probably estrogen-dependent, since oophorectomy [removal of the ovaries] is successful in this fraction of patients."

Dr. R. S. Mecklenburg, in a paper in the *New England Journal of Medicine,* underlined what Dr. Taylor had stated, when he commented on disappearance of both breast cancer and metastases (in a single case) after oophorectomy.

The pharmaceutical houses were alert to the opportunity these reports offered, for they suggested that an antiestrogen drug might be useful to women suffering from estrogen-dependent malignancies. It was used, and the research was reported in the *British Medical Journal,* by Dr. H. C. Ward. He observed regression (shrinkage) of the cancers in 60 percent of the women given 40 milligrams daily of tamoxifen, an antiestrogen compound. He showed that the improvement was definitely attributable to the drug, for, given half the dose, only 51 percent of the women responded. (Here is a good point to remind you that estriol is a *natural* antiestrogen substance, the manufacture of which in the body is dependent on the adequacy of your diet.)

Strangely, none of the researchers who have observed benefit from drugs or surgery used to reduce estrogen activity has evinced any interest in the use of antiestrogen measures *before* cancer appears. But there is one researcher who does focus on the efficiency with which the body produces impeded estrogen, rather than on the absolute estrogen level. Dr. H. M. Lemon, writing in the *Journal of the American Medical Association,* notes that higher urinary ratios of estriol to estrogen, associated with a decrease in the incidence of breast cancer, occur both in pregnancy, where estriol may be manufactured by the fetal liver, and after menopause. His current research is directed to the possibility of dosing women with concentrated estriol, in an effort to achieve a more desirable ratio between it and estrogen.

Again, it is strange that the concept of achieving that ratio via diet has not been entertained by any of these highly qualified researchers, which, perhaps, illustrates the physician's emphasis on medication and his tendency to neglect nutrition. At any rate, though Dr. Lemon's paper appeared in 1966, we find that same journal remarking (*eight* years later): "No conclusive data exist that relate administered steroidal estrogen with human breast or endometrial cancer." The escape hatch in that statement is the term "conclusive data." The editors are not saying that Lemon's research, and that of the hundreds of workers who preceded him, aren't evidence; they are saying that they've decided it isn't significant, and can be ignored. Which makes it poignant that the *JAMA* in 1976 thought it necessary to reassure frightened physicians who were asking if prescriptions for estrogen could become prima facie evidence of malpractice.

And while we're on the subject of this medical bible of the establishment, let me note that the *JAMA* has covered itself against the possibility that nutrition may one day be recognized as a factor in estrogen-dependent disorders, for it editorially remarked, a long time ago: "There are those who believe that diet plays a role in cystic disease of the breast, via hepatic degradation of estrogen. They, too, may be right." This salute to the interplay of liver function and diet and that of liver function and estrogen degradation is, unfortunately, an isolated incident in the literature of establishment medicine.

Continuing this sampling of the evidence which crystalized my conviction, gained from observing the reactions of thousands of women to improved diet, that nutrition is a neglected weapon against breast and uterine cancer, consider the statements made by Herbert H. Wotiz, Ph.D., at a function of the American Cancer Society. The scientist, a member of the biochemistry department of Boston University, proposed a lack of estriol or an overabundance of the more active estrogens as part of the complex of causes of breast cancer. He endorsed a test of estriol as a safe oral contraceptive—safe because it isn't carcinogenic and it competes with other forms of estrogen in the endometrial (uterine) cells. This statement is important to *you:* it means that estriol is picked up by the estrogen-receptor factor, which locks out the more active, carcinogenic form of the hormone. This is analogous to jamming a lock with the wrong key: no other key can enter.

How important the statement is may be gauged from the responses of rats to cancer-producing chemicals, with and without added doses of estriol. In the control animals, dosed with the chemical carcinogens, there was a 50 percent incidence of breast carcinomas, but when the animals were also given estriol, the incidence of mammary carcinoma was reduced to less than 10 percent and that was accomplished with a dose of estriol every two months. This report, originating with the May 31, 1976, issue of the *JAMA,* is another which emphasizes how important it is for you to use your nutrition to achieve a favorable ratio between estriol and estrogen in your body. The urgency increases if you have chronic cystic mastitis, for a report in the British journal *Lancet* (July 31, 1976) shows how the risk of breast cancer in such women is multiplied by 2½—meaning that of

733 women in whom chronic mastitis had been diagnosed, followed for a period of more than thirty years, 49 died from breast cancer, compared with an expected number of 18.8. And the excess risk of dying from breast cancer persisted for at least thirty years after chronic mastitis had been diagnosed.

The illusion of the postmenopausal woman that estrogen supplements are safer for her than for younger women, who are still producing the hormone, has been destroyed in a spate of papers in many journals. Typical are the statements made in a special communication to the *JAMA* (August 23, 1976):

> The estimated risk of acquiring endometrial cancer was 7.6 times higher for women who were treated with estrogens, and the risk increased with the length of time on the medication.

After seven years of estrogen treatment, the estimated risk was multiplied by a factor of nearly 14! Moreover, the danger was highest in patients who did *not* have conditions often identified with increased risk of endometrial cancer, such as obesity, diabetes, and hypertension. As an ironic and dismaying aspect of estrogen prescriptions, the medical journal described estrogens as sometimes prescribed for trivial reasons and yet taken over extended periods of time. About a *quarter* of the women had complained of hot flashes before the estrogen treatment was prescribed, and yet more than *half* the women had taken the hormone for more than three months—the average being about ten years. In the communication, it is noted that the use of estrogens for the treatment of menopause became popular in the 1960s, which, with the long delay intervening between insult and cancer, may mean that our women are now picking up the bill for years of a tragic mistake, which the article defines in this way: the risk of estrogen treatment is comparable to a pack-a-day smoker's chance of initiating lung cancer. But it is the smoker who does the calculating when he takes the risk!

While this chapter has concentrated on the estrogen-estriol profile in terms of building resistance to breast and uterine cancer, don't forget that female hormone is a versatile mischief-maker, for it also contributes to heart and blood vessel disorder, from myocardial infarction to thrombophlebitis. It increases blood triglycerides, which may help pave the way to hardening of the arteries; it can induce strokes. It also impairs carbohydrate tolerance, meaning that it can trigger a latent diabetes, stirs up endometriosis, and induces retention of water and salt, which is undesirable in normal women, threatening to those with hypertension.

If this chapter has sharpened your perspective, you are now prepared for a review of what you have learned thus far:

1. The body breaks down ovarian hormones of the estrogen type into estriol.

2. About 50 percent of that estriol production takes place in the liver.

3. The ability of the liver to effect the conversion is directly dependent upon the adequacy of the diet.

4. Research—my own and that of other observers—indicates that the "normal" American diet of "normal" women can be and often *is* inadequate to support maximum efficiency of that vital liver function.

5. Epidemiological evidence—the study of the cancer experience of other populations—shows clearly that the estriol/estrogen ratio is critical in determining susceptibility to breast cancer.

6. The conversion of estrogen into estriol not only lowers the body burden of estrogen, but also alters the estrogen/estriol ratio toward that obtaining in Oriental

women whose risk of breast cancer is 80 percent less than that of American and Canadian women.

After I wrote these lines, I read a text on breast cancer by an expert, Dr. George Crile, Jr., who describes another method of lowering estrogen levels: having your ovaries removed before you reach the age of forty. You do remember, don't you, my earlier remarks about the professor of preventive medicine who espoused removal of both of a healthy young woman's breasts to prevent malignancy? I prefer my way.

Though I have called this specialized use of nutrition "my way," I'm no longer alone in stressing the relationship of food to susceptibility to uterine and breast cancer. Other voices are joining—and some of what they are saying is misconceived and misleading. A recent example is the attempt to indict animal fat in the diet as a link with breast cancer. The flaw in the logic isn't apparent, particularly when the association seems strong: the American woman eats more animal fat than the Japanese woman, and is much more likely to develop cancer of the breast. Therefore, animal fat is the maker of malignancy.

Let me illustrate the flaw in that logic by repeating the details of an old experiment with chickens. Chickens aren't very intelligent, but they can be taught to obtain a grain of corn by pulling a string that opens a feeding tube. One rooster earned a place in scientific history because he happened to pull a feather from his tail before he tried pulling the string, and finding the sequence rewarding, he repeated it every time he wanted food.

That rooster's misinterpretation of cause and effect is one every scientist was taught to avoid. You don't use correlation to imply or demand causation; it merely suggests it with some degree of probability, which may be vanishingly small. If B always follows A, it doesn't prove that A causes B. If there are more neurotics, psychotics, and weirdos wherever there are more psychiatrists, it doesn't necessarily mean that psychiatrists drive you whacky. It simply means that psychiatrists gravitate to the urban areas where there are more people in need of treatment; and those in need tend to go to areas where help is available. In short, those who incautiously interpret cause-and-effect relationships can find themselves deciding that umbrellas cause rain to fall: after all, whenever they're in use, it's usually raining.

Unfortunately, that kind of thinking is being applied currently to explain how the Japanese woman's diet sustains her immunity to breast cancer. In the press in recent months, I've read indictments of the American woman's high intake of animal fat—which is much higher than the Japanese woman's—as causing her tendency to malignancies. It is possible but not probable that a single dietary factor is the variable in the equation of diet versus cancer. It is highly unlikely that fat intake has anything to do with the problem. That theory encounters diametrically opposed facts: for instance, the American black female consumes more fat than her white counterpart, but has less breast cancer; and there are a number of ethnic groups, worldwide, who should be riddled with such cancers but aren't, despite a *very* high intake of animal fat. One can point to Eskimo, Mongolian, and Masai women as examples. If anything, Eskimos of both sexes display a resistance to all types of cancer until they discard their ancestral diet, which is markedly high in fat, for the convenience of our foods. A physician who spent decades in treating Eskimos, and who actually lived with them, has said that he simply didn't see any cancer or others of the degenerative diseases which crowd our medical facilities.

The attempt to identify a deficiency or an oversupply of an isolated dietary factor as *the* cause of breast cancer must somehow fit in with a long list of variables which bear upon the incidence of the disease. Related to the rate of breast cancer in American women, for instance, will be not only the diet, but the age at first pregnancy, the number of pregnancies, the cancer history of the family, breastfeeding versus not breastfeeding, the age at the first menstruation, the age at menopause (whether natural or surgical), the presence or absence of cystic disease of the breast, and the exposure, if any, to estrogen treatment. While it is obviously impossible to link these variables with fat intake, it is pertinent to the thesis of this book that many of them ultimately involve the estrogen/estriol profile.

Since it's possible that you read and were impressed by the recent articles indicting dietary fat for breast cancer, it may be helpful if I briefly review the evidence for and against this concept, beginning by confessing and explaining a bias in my thinking. I don't believe that dietary animal fat is *the* factor (or even *a* factor) for the good reason that among the diets with which I have lowered the level of estrogenic activity in women, there is an effective one which is generously supplied with fat—more fat than the average woman is likely to consume. So, since the indictment of estrogen as a carcinogen is now very well documented and the case against fat rests largely on correlation interpreted as causation, I make no apologies for my preset judgment.

The suggestion was made a decade ago that there is a strong correlation between consumption of fats and oils, and death rates from cancer of the breast. The investigator proposed that this effect was really related to the cholesterol content of certain dietary fats, together with their property of raising blood cholesterol. If his thesis had proved valid, it would have been interesting to you and me, because cholesterol is the precursor substance from which the body makes estrogen. But the theory ran head on into the opposing fact of the low incidence of breast cancer in ethnic groups known to eat a high-fat diet.

The evidence from animal experiments is no more impressive. Rats on high intake of corn oil did become less resistant to drugs which cause breast cancer, but it was found that the oil enhanced the occurrence of the tumors only when it was fed *after* the carcinogenic chemical was given, not when fed before. This meant, of course, that the dietary history of fat intake had no relevance. It was also discovered that Vitamin E had a protective effect: animals given the high-fat diet plus the cancer-producing chemical plus the vitamin had a reduced incidence of breast cancer. Entirely apart from the fact that 50 percent of the food you eat has had some 90 percent of its Vitamin E removed in food processing, this observation of an anticarcinogenic effect of the vitamin does have some importance, and will be discussed later, but the research does nothing to strengthen the case against fat itself as a cause of breast cancer. Total substitution of vegetable fats for animal fats may be hazardous. The danger may derive from an insufficient supply of Vitamin E needed to protect such polyunsaturated fats from "rancidity" in the cells. This may explain an earlier reference to an anti-cancer effect of the vitamin in animal research with diets high in corn oil.

For a high-fat diet to have an effect which can be measured, the absolute amount of fat fed must be significant. (A reducing diet may contain a high *percentage* of fat, but the *amount* of it is small.) If there is a generous amount of fat in the animals' diet, they will tend to be obese—fat having a high caloric value. Since animal obesity itself has been linked with susceptibility to cancer, it is obviously impossible to separate the effects in such diets: is it the high intake of fat or the overweight it produces which enhances the risk of cancer? In any case, in human beings body weight and risk of breast cancer are not significantly correlated in any of the studies presently available. The only meaningful relationship, which I mentioned earlier in this chapter, derives from the fact that fat women tend to be overfed but malnourished—deficient in the nutritional factors needed to support the breakdown of estrogen.

There have been attempts to link two other dietary factors to breast cancer because Oriental women, so resistant to the disease, have better dietary supplies of selenium and iodine than do American women. These relationships may prove more tenable, for highly complex reasons. Selenium is related to the metabolism of Vitamin E, which I have already described as an anticancer factor, and iodine is related, of course, to thyroid function, which, as a member of the community of glands, is interrelated with the metabolism of estrogen. Again, I don't believe there is validity in any attempt to label iodine or selenium as *the* nutritional factor that bars breast cancer, but unlike fat intake, they may play a role.

And that brings us to the details of the nutrients which demonstrably tame the cancer-producing potential of the female hormone. In the next chapter, this nutritionist will attempt to guide you into an understanding of the Vitamin B Complex, protein, selenium, and iodine as armor against breast cancer, and excessive intake of sugar as a predisposing factor. Which makes the upcoming chapter the most important in the book. Permit me to illustrate its importance by means of a story:

The Spanish say God does not subtract from a man's appointed life-span the hours he spends in fishing. So it was that I bought a boat, and went fishing, sometimes fifty miles offshore—which displayed how much I trusted the mechanics at the marina, for I never had learned how to maintain and repair the motors. That is, not until I was caught in a violent squall in the Gulf Stream and the motors defied the laws of probability by quitting simultaneously. I then became a mechanic in a great hurry, managing to read the motor manual with the small boat threatening at any moment to capsize.

In the next chapter, I am asking you to do a smarter thing: to read the manual of nutrition now, when the sea is calm. I could tersely and without explanation list the nutritional steps to help prevent cancer, but I won't, because I know that you will more faithfully pursue the goal if you know what you are doing and why. My philosophy, based on nearly thirty years of experience with students, coincides with that of my professor of mathematics, who urged me not to memorize formulas. "Learn the concepts behind them, instead," he explained, "and you'll be able to derive the formulas at any time that you need them." So with you: if you master the concepts behind the recommendations this book makes, you will never impeach science by choosing the wrong foods—indeed, the correct choices will soon come by reflex, without conscious thought. Which is as it should be.

The chapter also has its complexities, for which, after the preceding explanation, I'll not apologize. In reading it, you'll become familiar with nutrients which not only offer anti-cancer effects, but also—as a delightful bonus—retard the aging process.

4

Star-Born Molecules that Protect against Cancer

The soil, which supports life, and the earth it covers are made of elements formed in stars long ago vanished. Since the depth of the topsoil is finite (and thinning), its building materials have been used over and over again, in untold thousands of generations of plant, animal, and man. So is it possible that within you are a few of the star-born molecules which once made Delilah, Cleopatra, or some Neanderthal woman.

The supply of nutrients in the soil is also finite, and when the drain upon it in intensive cultivation isn't compensated by good fertilization, it can become an uncertain source of some of the elements of nutrition which we need to support well-being. All this bears pointedly on our problems with such degenerative diseases as cancer of the breast, ovaries, and uterus.

It may not be chance correlation, then, that geographic differences in the incidence of these diseases are associated with differences in the selenium and iodine values in foods. Selenium is an antioxidant in the body, protecting the chromosomes from damage which can lead to cancer.

Iodine, as you probably know, is essential to thyroid function, but it may also play a role, directly or through its function in thyroid hormone, in susceptibility to breast cancer.

One government researcher believes that a low iodine intake may cause stimulation of the sex glands, with resulting elevation of estrogen production and, he adds, impairment of the process by which the body controls the activity of the hormone—a thesis linked to what we have been studying. I might add that it is axiomatic in medicine that high levels of estrogen tend to depress thyroid activity—as, of course, does iodine deficiency. It may not be coincidence, then, that geographic differences in the rate of breast, uterine, and ovarian cancer are inversely related to the iodine intake from the diet; i.e., the lower the iodine quota, the higher the cancer rate.

As an initial step toward protecting yourself, you should take the simple steps necessary to check your iodine intake, which is usually adequate if you are using iodized salt, or supplementing your diet with kelp or with a multiple mineral supplement containing a form of iodine. Tests of the thyroid gland itself will, of course, offer a clue to inadequate iodine intake. The physician has several sensitive tests for thyroid function, but there is also one you can perform at home, which will indicate if it is urgent to have your doctor follow up with laboratory tests. You simply place a thermometer in your armpit, with your arm at your side, before arising in the morning, and lie quietly for ten minutes. If your temperature falls below 97.8° F., a visit to your physician is in order, for your thyroid is likely to be underactive.

This test was devised by Dr. Broda Barnes, in years of research, and is surprisingly sensitive and reliable, though European physicians seem more familiar with it than American medical men. Should it confirm hypothyroidism, your doctor can prescribe small doses of the hormone, which, *if your diet is adequate*, may yield gratifying improvements in your ability to maintain normal weight and in the condition of your skin, nails, and hair, as well as added dividends in improved bowel function and resistance to colds, fatigue, and cold weather. If your diet isn't corrected, you won't respond. In fact, the administration of thyroid to a woman with a history of poor diet is irrational, and may actually cause worsening of her nutritional deficiencies. You are already familiar with one reason for this interrelationship, though you may not be aware of it. Poor nutrition allows estrogen levels in the blood to rise too high, and estrogen is antithyroid. If the estrogen levels aren't lowered by improvement of the diet, thyroid medication will obviously be ineffective. In fact, medical nutritionists have reported that many signs of hypothyroidism have disappeared, without administration of thyroid hormone, in response to improved nutrition.

Assuming that your thyroid gland is behaving normally, you can help to protect it with the diet that controls estrogen, with adequate intake of thiamin (Vitamin B_1) and with a minuscule iodine intake: about 100 micrograms daily. This term means a thousandth of a milligram, which is itself a thousandth of a gram, which is a thirtieth of an ounce. A microgram is the weight of a period made with a lead pencil. With what little things our functioning is determined!

The mention of thiamin (B_1) as a factor in thyroid function may puzzle you, for so far as the public is concerned, iodine has been described as *the* dietary factor on which this gland depends. Actually, intake of this vitamin is at least as important to the thyroid as is iodine and perhaps more so, because the effects of iodine deficiency are, at least to a point, reversible, but thiamin deficiency can cause irreversible drops in the efficiency of the gland. And, by way of illustrating the interaction of dietary factors, excessive sugar intake can cause thiamin deficiency. Other dietary errors can be involved, too. Some foods contain antithyroid factors and, if taken in excess, can cause trouble. These include cabbage, broccoli, brussels sprouts, and kale. One commonly used food which has an antithyroid effect is soy. This doesn't recommend, however, completely avoiding it or the cabbage family. It means using them but in reasonable quantities, particularly if there is a history of thyroid underactivity in the family. This is also true of the anti-gray-hair vitamin, PABA.

Selenium, appearing in nature as a gray crystal or a red powder, is as quixotic and contradictory a nutrient as any in the long list of our requirements, for in very small amounts it has been credited with preventing human cancer and in larger amounts it causes cancer in rats—though such an action in human beings has yet to be verified.* In fact, there is evidence of the opposite effect: protection against human cancer from adequate blood levels of selenium was demonstrated in a study in ten cities, where an almost perfect inverse correlation was found—meaning that low cancer rates were, 94 times per 100, associated with higher blood levels of the nutrient. The strength of this mathematical relationship is great, but that doesn't prove cause and effect. It *is* suggestive, though, for the good reason that we know of a property of selenium which may well be linked with higher resistance to cancer.

Among the roles of selenium in the body, there is one which protects you against the toxic effects of cadmium, a metal in foods that causes elevated blood pressure. If animal research is a guide to man's reactions, selenium also shields you from the toxicity of mercury in your foods. It increases the effectiveness of Vitamin E, which itself helps to protect against cancer. And as an antioxidant, not only does

*The same contradiction appears with X-ray exposure. Small doses, as given in mammography, are charged with causing breast cancer, while large doses, as you know, are used to treat the disease. This is also true of estrogens, which does *not* mean that a lifetime of a high burden of estrogen in the body is a boon.

selenium help to retard premature aging of the cells, but within them it protects DNA, the bearer of the genetic code. Since damage to DNA may disturb the inhibitors which control the cells' tendency to multiply—which unrestrained, could mean cancer—this action of selenium links it with protection against malignancies.

The term *antioxidant* may puzzle you, since most of us think of oxygen as a friend, not as an enemy. But with overactivity of oxygen in their eye tissues, premature babies develop retrolental fibroplasia, a disease which leads to blindness. With overactivity of oxygen in the cells, both premature aging and cancer are possible results, against which antioxidants protect. Nutrients which have this action are selenium, Vitamin E, Vitamin C, and the high-quality protein foods which supply sulfur—virtually a description of eggs. By fortunate happenstance, eggs are also a good source of selenium, and good sources—including brewer's yeast, garlic, and liver—are scarce. The sparsity of selenium in vegetable foods makes it desirable for vegetarians to supplement their diets with brewer's yeast, as a good source of this factor.

You have learned that the Vitamin B Complex is critical in the processes by which the liver controls estrogenic hormone activity. It is time now that you familiarize yourself with the known and unknown vitamins of this complex, for it not only helps to pull the fangs of estrogen, but builds resistance to the action of other carcinogens by supporting the ability of the liver to break them down and to convert them into harmless—or, at least, less harmful—compounds.

Such an action is illustrated perfectly in an experiment which yielded a significant indictment of hospital menus. A percentage of the animals fed scraps from hospital diets developed cancer, but the cancer rate dropped sharply when animals so fed were given supplements of brewer's yeast, which is a rich source of the Vitamin B Complex (and protein). The same result appeared in a Japanese experiment in which rats were dosed with a food additive known to cause cancer, but the addition of brewer's yeast to the animals' diet largely cancelled the carcinogenic effect.

Such results illustrate the double protection yielded by a generous supply of Vitamin B Complex—both against the carcinogenic effect of estrogen and that of food additives. They also point to a third possibility. Cancer-producing factors may interact with each other, with food, with pollutants in the environment, or with chemical substances normal to human metabolism. Such cross-reactions may be beneficial, reducing the cancer-causing potential, or they may increase the danger. No one knows, for we rarely study anything more than the isolated action of a single substance. Food additives are a classic example; we test them individually, but we swallow them together, to the tune of more than five pounds of such chemicals per person per year. Question: if you are a high-estrogen woman whose Vitamin B Complex intake is low and you, as all lipstick-using women often may, swallow a carcinogenic red dye daily, can the threat multiply, rather than add? Science says it multiplies, but we do have evidence that the better-fed woman is less likely to experience disaster. I must emphasize a very critical point. It is vital that you understand what I mean by a "better-fed" woman, for the meaning of the term is relative to your dietary history. If you have been deficient in Vitamin B Complex for a period of years, as exhibited in your estrogen level and your premenstrual and menstrual disturbances, your needs for these vitamins—to bring you back to normal and to keep you on an even keel—will forever be multiplied by a factor of 5 or even 10, as compared with the requirements of a woman who has always eaten properly. Tissue which has suffered dietary insult will recover, but it remembers the transgressions. For example: it may take five years of average American diet to convert your menstrual cycle into a nightmare. After we correct the diet and eliminate the menstrual disturbances, it may take only two months of poor diet to awaken all the old symptoms. Under the microscope the tissues show no change, but they remember, implacably.

There is a second critical point: every nutritionist is painfully aware of the effectiveness of stress in negating the benefits of improved diet. One sees a woman with classical symptoms of deficiency: she has a beefy red tongue which is painfully cracked, cracks at the corners of her mouth, dry skin, brittle nails, dry hair, excessive fatigability, and, let's say, cystic mastitis. Under the guidance of a medical nutritionist, her symptoms fade gradually as she eats a better diet, takes food supplements, and receives vitamins by injection. At the moment when all the symptoms seem about to disappear, she encounters a personal crisis—a divorce, the loss of a child, a devastating disappointment in her love life—and, even while the successful nutritional treatment is still in progress, every one of her symptoms flares up. The history emphasizes the interplay of glandular and nervous system functions with nutritional needs.

The Vitamin B Complex comprises a group of vitamins which tend to accompany each other in foods; hence the term *complex*. Many of the functions of these vitamins overlap, yet each factor has its own roles in the chemistry of the body and one cannot replace another. Often the B vitamins are components of enzyme systems, and it may be that the antiestrogen effect derives from one of these enzymes, as yet unidentified. The last phrase tells you that there are factors of the Vitamin B Complex we have not yet isolated and chemically identified, though we know they are there, and that their actions do not derive from the known vitamins of this group.

Included in the Vitamin B Complex are these identified nutritional factors:

Thiamin (Vitamin B_1)
Riboflavin (Vitamin B_2)
Biotin*
Niacin, niacinamide (Vitamin B_3)
Pyridoxin (Vitamin B_6)
Pantothenic acid (pantothenol)
Para-aminobenzoic acid (PABA)
Folic acid
Inositol
Choline
Pangamic acid (Vitamin B_{15})
Hydroxycobalamin, cyanocobalamin (Vitamin B_{12})
Orotic acid (Vitamin B_{13})

The unknown factors of the Vitamin B Complex puzzle the layman. The adjective seems to have a built-in contradiction: if they're unknown, how is their presence evidenced? A change from "unknown" to "chemically unidentified" would probably clarify matters, but to illustrate how we know they exist: There is an antifatigue factor in liver, which enormously increases the physical endurance of animals. Doses of all the known vitamins in liver, singly or in combination, don't yield the effect, which means, obviously, that in liver there is a factor—never seen, chemical structure unestablished—different from all the known nutrients in that fine food. The reasoning process is no different from that used by the nuclear physicist, who constantly works with unknown atomic particles, often can't isolate them, but can demonstrate what they're *not* and what their behavior is.

*It is sometimes puzzling that some vitamins have a chemical name while others have that *and* a letter and a number, as in Vitamin B_1. The explanation is simple. Before their chemical identity was established, vitamins were obviously of unknown structure. Letters and numbers were therefore assigned to them. After they were identified chemically—and made synthetically—the letter-number system was discarded. In later research, vitamins were chemically identified shortly after their existence was recognized, and these never received a letter or a number.

We know of an antianemia substance in liver, which is distinct from such other blood-building factors as copper, iron, protein, and Vitamin B_{12}. There is a progrowth factor there, too, which hasn't been identified, though its action in animals has been demonstrated. There is a substance in liver which is antithyroid, exactly as there is an antiestrogen factor, which may be an elusive enzyme which is vitamin-dependent. All this is not academic, for it explains why the supplementing aimed at control of estrogen activity should include a significant amount of liver. Here the animal experiments fail us and the reactions of women become the necessary criteria, for in the rat, thiamin (B_1) and riboflavin (B_2) are critical in helping the liver to break down estrogen, but in the human being others of the B vitamins are involved, including the elusive antiestrogen factor best supplied by desiccated (dried) whole raw liver.

After watching the responses of women to supplements of the Vitamin B Complex for the past twenty-five years, I have been able to identify two known vitamins which are directly involved in supporting liver degradation of estrogen. Ironically, most multiple-vitamin and B Complex supplements supply lip-service amounts of these vitamins, or none at all. The manufacturers have good excuses. For one thing, the nutrition establishment still doesn't recognize them as "essential in human nutrition"—a recognition long overdue. For another, the public and the professions are unaware of their importance to liver degradation of estrogen. And the postulated requirement for both is so large, as compared with other vitamins, that space limitations make it very difficult to incorporate all the other vitamins, plus significant amounts of *inositol* and *choline,* in any tablet or capsule of less than horse-pill size. In a few brands, fortunately, the problem has been solved and both vitamins are available separately, in tablet or capsule form; fortunately, because a Vitamin B Complex supplement without them has a much reduced antiestrogen effect. This is logical, for both factors are involved in fat metabolism, and estrogens are fat-soluble hormones; and both factors have long been known to have important beneficial effects on the liver. All this doesn't mean that the other B vitamins, known or unknown, don't play a part in control of estrogen, but inositol and choline are key factors.

Earlier, when I noted that I learned more about nutrition from the veterinarian journals than from those published for physicians, I wasn't jesting. All animal husbandry schools include in their courses a great deal of instruction in (animal) nutrition, while there are many medical schools which don't teach the subject at all, or give grossly inadequate time to it. So it was that I learned of a proestrogen factor of the Vitamin B Complex from an article on the nutritional needs of young chickens. When estrogen is administered to chicks, the oviduct, which might loosely be compared with the human uterus, increases in size thirtyfold. If the chick is deficient in folic acid, the increase is only fourfold. An indirect reflection of this interrelationship became clear when it was discovered that birth control pills which contain estrogen cause a folic-acid deficiency in women. Later observations prove the same effect of the Pill on Vitamin B_6 and Vitamin B_{12}. These actions certainly demonstrate the interplay of female hormone with many factors of the Vitamin B Complex.

In research in clinical nutrition, when I directed the program at the Shaler Lawton Foundation, we repeatedly observed that women given large doses of folic acid frequently commented on increased swelling and tenderness of the breasts in the premenstrual week. This, of course, reflected a heightened response to estrogen and confirmed the findings in the chick experiment. The same action sometimes occurred with another B vitamin, para-aminobenzoic acid (PABA). This was logical, for PABA is part of the molecule of folic acid, and probably the active entity in the interplay of that vitamin with estrogen.

You should now have a perspective on nature's system of checks and balances in nutrition. The Vitamin B Complex supplies two factors which heighten the estrogen response and two which help to depress the activity of the hormone. This doesn't mean that women should not use a vitamin supplement containing folic acid or PABA, or a diet supplying needed quantities of the two nutrients. It simply means that the everyday supplement, used for diet insurance, shouldn't supply high doses of the two. Conversely, this research demands a generous supply of choline and inositol in both diet and supplements, plus the use of dried liver to supply, if possible, a meaningful intake of the preformed antiestrogen liver factor. In Chapter 7, where I provide diets to meet the needs peculiar to women, I also describe in detail what the supplements should provide.

There is a story of a man who bought a very expensive car, which gave him an infinite amount of trouble. He went back to the salesman and said: "Tell me again all the good points of this car—what you said before I bought it." With a similar philosophy, let me justify all the nutritional complexities I have inflicted upon you, by reminding you of some of the dividends I have seen in women who have shaped their nutrition to tame the female hormone. Cystic mastitis has improved or disappeared. In a few cases, endometriosis has responded. In two cases, uterine fibroid tumors shrank and in one, they disappeared. In thousands of women, premenstrual tension has lessened or vanished, and in more thousands, menstruation has shortened by about 40 percent, from five days to three. In innumerable women, other premenstrual symptoms—breast cysts, water retention with weight gain, hysteria, depression, anxiety, etc.—have lessened or disappeared.

And keep in mind the central thesis of this book: dietary control of estrogen activity is control of a cancer-producing hormone. Instead of removing healthy breasts because they are a target for estrogen; instead of removing ovaries and uteri because they are the producers of estrogen, I advocate placing nutritional brakes on the activity of the hormone. I still like my way better. Nor is mine a solitary voice. Consider this quotation, from "Nutritional Therapy of Endocrine [glandular] Disturbances" by M. S. Biskind, M.D., in *Vitamins and Hormones*, Volume 4 (New York: Academic Press, 1946):

> It seems likely that regressions in the growth of mammary carcinomas in animals, observed following administration of yeast extract and riboflavin, may have been mediated through enhancement of the estrogen-inactivating function of the liver. Since, however, the development of a malignant tumor represents a qualitative and, for the most part, irreversible change in the tissue affected, nutritional therapy would in practice be of value mainly in the prevention of preneoplastic [precancerous] lesions. As related to those produced by excess estrogen, the maintenance of normal hepatic [liver] function appears to be paramount.

Note the date of that paper: 1946—thirty years ago. Since then, nearly a million American women have died of breast cancer. Did their diets support optimal liver function? Did anyone ask? Did anyone care? I know of someone who did. Hearing one of my broadcasts on the subject, a brother of Dr. Biskind, himself a physician, wrote to me to say: "It is good to hear on the air nutritional truths as we know them and teach them to our patients."

There is an arithmetic which sets the odds for and against your remaining a healthy woman, for at this moment there are 7 million American women who are free of breast cancer, but will develop it in their lifetime. That is one in every fifteen women. During any working day, every three minutes and twenty seconds another woman has been staggered to learn that she has breast cancer, but at that, she may be better off than the 245,000 American women who have the disease and don't know it. These are the statistics which drive physicians into "preventing cancer" by removing healthy breasts or ovaries. (Less forgivable, as you will learn in the next chapter, is the philosophy of the physician who proposes to make continued doses of estrogen safe by performing hysterectomies on all postmenopausal women, though he grants that the procedure is a little impractical.)

Because important actions of nutrition in preventing cancer have been totally neglected for more than thirty years, this book was written. To this point, it has emphasized the usefulness of improved diet in depriving estrogen of its carcinogenic fangs. In the next chapter, it will be shown that this concept will serve to unify a number of variables in the incidence of breast cancer which seem in no way linked. Added to the concept will be another an equally neglected action of nutrition: raising the natural immunological defenses of the body, both in the prevention and the treatment of cancer. For this technique, we are indebted to Dr. Linus Pauling.

5

A Cascade of Clues, a Deluge of Disasters

If you hold a teaspoonful of sugar in your closed fist, you will promptly lose strength in the other arm. I can demonstrate this—not only with sugar, but with an unlit cigarette butt—but don't ask for an explanation. Students of the nervous system and muscle function (kinesiologists) will take years to collect, classify, and understand such observations, and more years to fit them all into a unified theory.

In much the same position are those who study the variables linked with the incidence of breast, uterine, and ovarian cancer. Even analysis of a single variable can be frustrating. Why is wet ear wax associated with susceptibility to breast cancer and dry ear wax with higher resistance? Diet could easily be a factor, but so could glandular function, and it could also involve an interaction between the two. Our endocrinologists (gland specialists) aren't trained in nutrition, as graduates of foreign medical schools are. One finds a German medical text, for instance, remarking that between dietary factors and hormones there is a state of co- and counterplay, the actions so intermixed that a deficiency of one may be reflected only in an imbalance of the other.

Such a viewpoint is largely alien to American medical thinking, which tends to view the glands as if in a vacuum, except in the case of the thyroid's dependence on iodine.

Breast cancer is less frequent in warm climates, but before you assign a preventive effect of heat, humidity, or sunshine, consider that breast cancer is also rarer among Oriental women, including those who live in *cold* climates. If you turn to heredity as an explanation, you are then confronted with the Oriental woman's increased susceptibility when she deserts her native diet.

Why does the danger of developing the disease increase as women climb higher on the socioeconomic ladder? Why does age make a difference, not only the woman's age, but how old she was when she bore her first child? Why are Jewish women more susceptible, and black women less?

It has been said that any researcher who attempts to fully understand the functioning of just one type of bacteria in our large, germ-laden bowels should be gently led away to a mental institution. Considering the number of variables which appear to influence the incidence of cancer, we can preserve sanity only by limiting the number of those we simultaneously juggle, or by attempting to find a factor, somewhere in the background, common to them all. One of these is the level of female hormone activity in *susceptible* women. The adjective is emphasized for a good reason: it takes more than an insult to produce a disease. It also requires a hospitable host. Estrogen activity must fall on a receptive target to work mischief. You may have in your mouth now a few of the bacteria which cause trench mouth, but not have the disease: the "soil" (the mouth environment) is rich enough in oxygen to deny the bacteria a foothold. The analogy is mixed but the thinking is accurate.

So it is with the level of female hormone activity: it can be appraised intelligently only when there is also consideration of the woman's ability to produce the inactivated (estriol) form of the hormone. This is the background for research which was a joint effort of the departments of public health at Harvard University and the University of Hawaii, together with the department of obstetrics and gynecology at the University of Melbourne, Australia. They began their research with the premise that young women whose excretion of estriol is low are high risks for breast cancer. They were aware that breast-cancer rates of Oriental women living in Hawaii are lower than those of white women, but substantially higher than those of women in Asia. They therefore measured ratios of estrogen to estriol in the urines of Chinese, Japanese, and Caucasian women in Hawaii, and compared them with those of women in Japan and China. They concluded that there is a definite association between the estriol/estrogen ratio in the urine and the risk of breast malignancy, their report emphasizing that a low ratio of estriol to estrogen invites the disease. There is no discussion in their paper of the diets of the women as the factor in determining that ratio. But if it isn't the diet, what does change when the Oriental woman moves from Asia to this country, alters her estriol/estrogen ratio in so doing, and dilutes her resistance to breast cancer?*

Once diet is considered, it becomes possible to unify what otherwise appears to be an array of totally independent factors which elevate or lower resistance to breast and uterine cancer. Consider, as an example, the early onset of menstruation, which is linked to breast cancer because the disease appears more frequently in those whose menstrual cycles began earlier. But the onset of menstruation is di-

*The pioneering research of the Biskinds in the role of diet in liver degradation of estrogen was performed before the conversion of estrogen into estriol was recognized. Those interested in the chemistry of the conversion will find it discussed in *Proceedings of the Society for Clinical Research*, 1972, vol. 20, p. 796, and in the *Journal of Surgical Oncology*, 1972, vol. 3, p. 255, both by H. M. Lemon. In the latter paper, Dr. Lemon identifies the high level of urinary estriol excretion in healthy, premenopausal, nonpregnant Asian women, and links it with their significant resistance to breast cancer.

rectly related to the achievement of a critical body weight, and that, of course, is very much affected by the diet. So it is that excessive consumption of foods like sugar, which not only stimulates weight gain but prods the glandular activities which influence height gain, may trigger an early menstruation. The mischief is compounded, since a high intake of such a poor food will impair the ability of the liver to properly regulate estrogen activity.

Could we study variations in diet as women go higher in socioeconomic classes, we might find as direct a dietary influence, too. It is, however, difficult to generalize about diet. The phrase "we are what we eat" is a half truth, for as Dr. Roger Williams aptly suggested, we are what we eat, absorb, *and* utilize—functions never quite the same in two individuals, even of the same ancestry. Then, too, accuracy in appraisal of "average" food intake is difficult to achieve. I *know*, for I struggled with such a study as part of the requirements for my doctorate degree. We write about an "average" intake of about 100 pounds of sugar per person per year, but the average is made up of those who fall above it as well as those who fall below, and I have assayed many diets containing a health-jeopardizing total of more than 180 pounds in the yearly ration. It is the same reliance on averages that led cancer researchers to believe that excessive fat intake, largely from meat, is responsible for the American woman's susceptibility to breast malignancy. But there are two gross errors in that estimate. It rests on the fallacious belief that you eat what you buy, which simply isn't true. You may carefully trim the excess fat from your lamb chops or steak; your sister may not. Then, too, the figures for meat consumption are frequently based on the carcass weight before trimming, but if you've ever bought a side of beef, you well know the significant loss of weight encountered in the trimming of bone and waste. This, coupled with cooking shrinkage, drops the American per capita intake of meat far below the level the U.S. Department of Agriculture recommends for a good diet, and certainly much less than that consumed by such ethnic groups as the African Masai—who, if animal fat intake were a significant cause of cancer, would long ago have vanished. Again, the average intake of meat derives from those whose consumption falls below it and from those who raise it by eating steak twice a day.

Turning from excessive intake of a dietary factor to deficiency, the association of inadequate diet with decreased resistance to malignancies is well documented. Iodine deficiency may lead to an underactive thyroid and ultimately to a goiter, and goiters have been clearly associated with an increased risk of breast cancer. Similarly, recognizable thyroid underactivity has been demonstrated in 10 percent of the women with another type of cancer (endometrial). This brings us back to estrogen, for there is experimental evidence that thyroid underactivity goes hand in hand with high estrogen levels. The researchers who have studied this relationship believe other hormones may be involved, but some of them squarely indict iodine deficiency as causing raised estrogen levels and, to compound the mischief, an unfavorable ratio of estriol to estrogen.

On the basis of this involvement of thyroid deficiency in cancer, a few cancer specialists have recommended the use of thyroid hormones as a preventive measure against *recurrence* of breast cancer, but as a nutritionist I'll cast my vote for adequate intake of iodine and Vitamin B_1 (thiamin) *now*, while you're well and your thyroid is presumably efficient. Which is a vote for a thyroid test—whether it's done with the temperature method, the laboratory methods, or both (see Chapter 4).

The prescriptions for estrogen to control menopausal symptoms have been directly blamed for a 35 percent increase in uterine cancer in a California study. Though the layman would expect physicians to expunge the hormone from their armamentariums after such disaster reports, this is not the way the medical mind operates, and one finds physicians still defending the practice of estrogen treatment "to give menopausal and postmenopausal women a better quality of life." (The corollary, which seems to be ignored, is a better quality of death.) Faced with this problem, a medical editorialist (*Lancet*, December 6, 1975), accepting the validity of the risk of heightened incidence of cancer in postmenopausal women who take estrogen, suggested that "the only possible recommendation is that all candidates for long-term estrogen replacement should have a hysterectomy—not a very attractive prospect if the eventual aim is treatment of entire populations." His philosophy seems of the same vintage as that of the physician who removed the young girl's normal breasts to prevent genetically determined breast cancer, and that of the surgeon who mentioned prevention by removal of the ovaries before the age of forty.

There are, obviously, two other alternatives: let the patient decide whether she will choose sweats and flushes in place of a risk of breast cancer, or call on the medical nutritionist for prescriptions of nutrients which may control menopausal disturbances. (Vitamin E, to cite one, has been known to control these symptoms in some women, the first report having appeared in a medical journal in 1949.) I should add that the efficacy of estrogen treatment is open to serious question. Really competent, large-scale controlled tests of the hormone in the management of menopausal symptoms are virtually nonexistent; which is disgraceful, considering the millions of women arbitrarily dosed with this carcinogenic hormone for their sweats and flushes, which it may help, and for their nervousness and dry skin, which the FDA says it won't help. I should also add that nutritional treatment for the menopause should begin twenty years before it appears.

In a grateful change from crisis medicine and its dangers to preventive medicine, researchers have examined the daughters of women with breast cancer, finding that these young, still healthy girls have the high levels of estrogen and other hormones characteristic of their mothers. These scientists exhibited none of the intellectual bankruptcy that leads to such suggestions as removing breasts and uteri in order to deprive estrogen of receptive targets. Instead, Dr. Brian Henderson, in a paper delivered at a recent conference on cancer at the University of Southern California School of Medicine, emphasized childhood diet as the possible trigger for these threatening levels of carcinogenic hormones. What price junk foods? And where in the long history of our battle against cancer will be the place of home economics teachers who have eulogized overprocessed foods and taught their students how to base recipes on them—not to mention the registered dietitians who dispense them to the hospitalized who need the best of nutrition?

I mentioned in Chapter 4 the paradoxical treatment of breast cancer with high doses of estrogen, as puzzling to the layman as the use of irradiation, which can cause cancer, in treating it. Here it is pertinent that the National Cancer Institute has reported that women treated with estrogen for breast cancer may, as a result, fall prey to uterine cancer. That principle also applies to the cytotoxic drugs, the chemotherapy which largely dominates present-day cancer treatment; I have just read the first report that administration of these chemicals for a type of cancer may be followed, years later, by an increased risk of other types of malignancy.* This came as no new idea, for in a personal communication to me, a cancer researcher whose studies in natural immunological resistance to malignancy I shall later detail, remarks: "Both chemotherapy and irradiation lower natural resistance to the disease."

I referred before to one of the puzzling variables in the occurrence of breast cancer, the age at which a woman has

*R. Hoover et al., *Lancet*, April 24, 1976, pp. 885–86.

her first child, for those who do so at an early age are more resistant to the disease. If you investigate this relationship, you find that once again you are dealing with the ancient enemy, estrogen. Compared with childless women, those who had their first babies when young tend to have a higher ratio of estriol to estrogen. The researchers who established this conclude that estrogen metabolism, as reflected in the estriol ratio, is in fact a determinant of the breast-cancer risk; that comment will tell you why I remarked that among many of these apparently unrelated factors in cancer risk, a unifying thread can be found.

Before we detour to the history of another nutrient which has promise both in the prevention and the treatment of cancer, let me pause to correct a possible false impression of the philosophy of this book. My obvious indignation when surgical mutilation is substituted for nutritional prevention of malignancy should not be interpreted as a facet of generic hostility to all physicians. Not so; I've been an officer of a large medical society, a director of another, and a founding fellow of a third, and thus I am aware of, and even on a first-name basis with, hundreds of physicians, dedicated and caring, to whom the integrity of the body is sacrosanct and who are keenly conscious of the importance of nutrition, and practice it as an effective and essential component of preventive medicine.

The hostility does exist and does flare, though, when I encounter the kind of medical philosophy that was applied to the wife of a distant relative of mine. She had a radical mastectomy, followed by an oophorectomy (removal of the ovaries to bring down the estrogen level—sound familiar?) Despite the surgery and the postoperative irradiation and chemotherapy, she is still in trouble. I answered her husband's desperate call for help by suggesting that he talk to the physician about massive doses of Vitamin C, which have been found to extend the life expectancy of even terminal cancer patients. The physician was both obstructive and indignant. His immediate response was: "How do you know there won't be side effects from large doses of Vitamin C?" Do you suppose he is unaware of the grave side effects of the corticosteroids (cortisone-type drugs) and cell-killing medication he has prescribed for this patient? When asked what possible side reactions Vitamin C might cause, he answered: "I don't know—but there could be some." He *could* know; there are detailed published reports of long-term observation of megavitamin doses of Vitamin C, not only in cancer, but in numerous other serious diseases, and *no* significant side reactions have been recorded, even in patients so dosed with the vitamin for five to ten years. He could talk with some of the surgeons who are routinely giving the vitamin to men who have had prostatectomies (removal of the prostate gland) for cancer.

The doctor's second response was: "How do you know Vitamin C won't interfere with the chemotherapy?" (His patient isn't getting better on that, and he must know it.) His third response was unspoken, but clearly audible. He was really saying: "How dare you assume that I'm not infallible?" He maintained his dignity and his cloak of infallibility, and his patient was deprived of very possible, real benefit from a harmless vitamin.

With that as a preface, let's discuss what is known about the responses of cancer patients to large doses of Vitamin C, and what such responses denote in possibilities of cancer prevention.

The body obviously does have built-in defenses against cancer, whereby we probably develop and stamp it out daily—if we're healthy and well nourished. Let's take a look at the evidence for that statement:

1. Transplants of cancer cells to the tissues of healthy people are rejected; transplants of cancer cells to cancer

patients take hold. The obvious conclusion: there is a defense mechanism which is efficient in normal people and ineffective in those with cancer.

2. Schizophrenics have a puzzling, high resistance to cancer. They have in their blood a protein—alpha 2 macroglobulin—which may battle the disease exactly as antibodies battle specific infections.

3. When drugs which depress the natural immunological mechanisms of the body are given to patients receiving organ transplants, a shockingly high percentage of the patients are likely to develop cancer. What rejects transplants, rejects cancer. Negate it and the transplant is accepted, and so is cancer.

4. There are well-documented cases of patients definitely known to have cancer, who recovered from the disease without treatment.

If you add those four observations, you are forced to the conclusion that the healthy body has the capacity to prevent cancer from gaining a foothold while that capacity has been vitiated or totally impaired in cancer patients, for any of a number of possible reasons.

Acting on that theory, investigators have sought the factors in the blood that may bar—or encourage—cancer. Three, in fact, have been found, an anticancer factor and two more which block its action, but this research has, as usual, received no encouragement from a cancer establishment wedded to the concepts of crisis medicine with its use of toxic drugs and irradiation. That establishment, proprietors of a cancer industry involving some $25 billion a year, has been similarly underwhelmed by recent reports, originating with research by Dr. Linus Pauling, that Vitamin C in substantial doses prolongs the lives of terminal cancer patients and appears in some actually to have caused the disease to disappear. This, of course, means that the vitamin may have preventive value—for what nutrition cures, it ordinarily prevents or at least mitigates. It also invites trial of the vitamin therapy in early rather than in terminal cases, where it logically should produce even happier results. As a commentary on our drug-oriented culture, let me observe that Dr. Pauling has been compelled to search for research funds which would be easily available if he were studying the action of a highly toxic, cell-destroying chemical.

Although Pauling's research has been greeted as if the use of Vitamin C in the treatment of malignancy is a new aspect of his catholic interests in the vitamin's actions, the fact is that reports of the usefulness of the vitamin in the treatment of cancer go all the way back to the 1940s, mostly in the European medical literature. Those reports were allowed to gather dust, exactly as were those concerning Vitamin B Complex and its actions on estrogen metabolism. But from the 1950s on, there were repeated observations of deficiency in Vitamin C in the white blood cells of patients with cancer. These are the cells which the body uses to destroy both bacteria and alien cells, which would, of course, include cancer. One physician, a surgeon, did heed that research. He is Dr. Ewan Cameron, who had operated on many cancer patients and was strongly motivated to find a better modality than the scalpel for controlling the disease. He was aware that malignancies produce an enzyme which attacks the "cement" that glues normal cells together, making it easier for the invading cancer to penetrate the tissues. Could that intercellular cement be strengthened to bar the invasion? He tried doses of hormones and other drugs, without success, and then his attention was drawn to Vitamin C when Pauling described its specific action in strengthening that glue. (For the technically minded, the vitamin actually helps to increase the synthesis of collagen fibrils, which are essential to the "cement.") In 1971, Dr. Cameron inaugurated trials of large doses of Vitamin C, 10,000 milligrams daily, in patients with far advanced cancer. (It is customary to attempt new therapies only on patients who are demonstrated victims of cancer so far progressed that orthodox treatments can no longer help.)

Cameron and his associates reported that Vitamin C reduced pain so effectively that narcotics were no longer needed for patients who had required large doses. That paper was followed by another, detailing the responses of the initial group of fifty patients with advanced cancer. Then came a report on a patient who appeared to recover completely from cancer, thanks to large doses of the vitamin, only to relapse when the vitamin therapy was stopped, and to recover again when the dose of Vitamin C, 12,500 milligrams daily, was resumed.

Pauling and Cameron now joined forces, studying 100 patients with advanced cancer who, when it was apparent that ordinary treatments no longer held promise for them, were given 10 grams of Vitamin C daily. The experiment was carefully controlled—there were 10 control patients of the same age, sex, and with the same type of cancer, to match each of the sufferers treated with the vitamin. The results are very promising, for the vitamin-treated patients have lived four times as long as the controls. Eighteen of the 100 patients treated with Vitamin C are living, while all the controls—the entire 1,000—have died. Moreover, sixteen of these eighteen show no evidence of cancer. The most significant lengthening of survival time occurred in patients with cancer of the colon. Second were those with breast cancer. In some of these patients, left without hope after failure to obtain help with surgery, chemotherapy, irradiation, or hormones, Vitamin C therapy converted days of survival, in the control group, to months and years of survival in the Vitamin C-treated patients. The terminal breast cancer cases, all veterans of the ineffectiveness of standard treatments, responded to Vitamin C by living 5.75 times longer than the average of the women in the control group. An elderly woman with cancer of the ovary responded to

Vitamin C by surviving almost six times longer than matching control patients with the same type of cancer. A fifty-year-old woman, terminal with breast cancer, survived four and a half years, while the matching patients in the control group, treated conventionally without the Vitamin C, lived an average of eighty-three days. This harmless vitamin therapy turned days of survival into months, and in many cases, years. Moreover, it significantly reduced pain, lessening the dependence of the patients on drugs.

These results in terminal cases urgently plead for a trial of the treatment in less advanced cancer, and such research is under way. It's obvious that the strengthening of the intercellular cement isn't the explanation for the response to Vitamin C treatment—not in terminal cases, which, by definition, are those where the cancer had already invaded so much of the body that the patient is dying. It is apparent that the vitamin must be increasing the body's capacity for resistance, via its stimulation of the white blood cells, those guardians of the body. Cancer patients, Pauling has observed, have a much greater requirement for Vitamin C than normal, healthy patients. The heightened need obviously derives from the effort the body makes to mobilize its resources when under stress. A colleague in the International Academy of Preventive Medicine advises me that a strong emotional stress can cause the body to utilize Vitamin C by the thousands of milligrams. You can imagine how that is multiplied when a cancer is draining one's resources.

Surely your reaction in reading this must match mine when I read the details of the Cameron-Pauling study in the *Proceedings of the National Academy of Sciences* (October, 1976). The experiment with terminal patients augurs well for the ongoing research with those with early cancer, but what might Vitamin C do to *prevent* cancer? There are already some epidemiological studies which point to the answer to that question. One involves gastrointestinal cancer, studied in a group of some 30,000 people. It revealed significantly lower rates of such cancers in those with high intakes of Vitamin C and vegetables. There are two other studies which clearly show that the death rate (including cancer deaths) for people fifty years and older is lower when the blood levels of Vitamin C are higher. One of these showed that the death rate for those on high intake of Vitamin C was only 40 percent of that for the subjects with a low intake. E. Cheraskin, professor of oral medicine at the University of Alabama Medical School, has published such findings too, involving a smaller group of subjects, and showing that the age at death is greater when blood levels of Vitamin C are higher, or, to reverse that, that you die younger when your blood is lower in the vitamin.

Many of us in the field of nutrition, Pauling included, have pointed out that you can't achieve high blood levels of Vitamin C with the 45 milligrams the government recommends as the "allowance for people in ordinary good health." Pauling is convinced that this low intake yields "ordinary poor health." Here you might be interested in learning that the Funk and Wagnalls Encyclopedia defines *health* as "a state of optimal well-being—never achieved." If it's never achieved, to whom does the recommendation of 45 milligrams of Vitamin C daily apply?

Man is one of but a few species unable to synthesize Vitamin C for themselves, and thereby dependent on environmental sources. The hamster, the guinea pig, the fruit-eating bat, the bulbul, and man are among those sharing this disability. At some point in our evolutionary history, we lost the enzyme which makes body synthesis of Vitamin C possible. Since the nutrient was available from other sources—fruits and vegetables—the mutation wasn't fatal. However, all the creatures capable of synthesizing Vitamin C make far more, per pound of body weight, than our government suggests for us. If we were able to manufacture Vitamin C as most other creatures do, a 150-pound man would synthesize more than 2,000 milligrams daily. And if man followed the biochemical pattern of other creatures, he would, if placed under stress, raise that Vitamin C output by a very large factor, the 2,000 milligrams rising to approximately 13,000. Viewed against that background, 45 milligrams of Vitamin C daily becomes ridiculously low—barely adequate to avoid life-threatening deficiency for some people—and Pauling's estimate of the range of requirement, from 250 milligrams to about 2,500 milligrams daily, no longer seems astronomically high. (Just by way of comparison, goats synthesize about 13,000 milligrams of Vitamin C daily.) Pauling is aiming at superhealth; the government figure is targeted on avoiding scurvy, the prelethal stage of deficiency. In terms of possible cancer prevention, in terms of reduced incidence of illnesses ranging from colds to allergy, in terms of heightened resistance to infection, both viral and bacterial—at which level would you wish to peg your Vitamin C intake? Enough to avoid scurvy and no more?

Not at all by coincidence, the factors in nutrition that raise resistance to cancer are all antioxidants, and these are also the factors which delay aging. Some of them you've already encountered: Vitamin E and selenium, for example. Add to the list Vitamin C, and finish it with the high-quality proteins that supply sulfur-containing amino acids, which I cited before as a virtual description of eggs. Add the Vitamin B Complex to aid liver function in control of estrogen. But you don't "eat" Vitamin B Complex or sulfur-containing amino acids: you assemble a diet adequate in these factors and you preserve the enjoyment of eating, for no compromise is necessary between fulfilling the pleasures of the palate and the needs of the organism. Which explains the menu-planning suggestions given in this book. I have included them because I suspect you need help in mastering the art of choosing foods you like which also like you.

6

Why a "Well Nourished" Woman Often Isn't

Observing that I was rubbing my forehead, the bright little girl, sitting next to me on the jet, solicitously asked if I had a headache. When I said I did, she offered to pray for me. She briefly closed her eyes and bowed her head, and then told me: "God said to take two aspirins, and if you don't feel better, call Him in the morning."

She was a child of our pharmaceutically orientated culture, in which there is a magic, fast-acting pill for everything: depression, anxiety, euphoria, sleeping, waking up, depressing appetite, stimulating appetite. . . . And from that background emerges a public anticipating that nutrition, too, has its magic pills that yield instant relief or, in the case of this book, immediately heightened resistance to cancer. That expectation has been voiced in the literally millions of letters I've received, which follow this pattern: "I've been sick for twenty years. I've tried internal medicine, psychiatry, gynecology, chiropracty, kinesiology, transcendental meditation, and hypnosis. No relief. Could you supply a diet and some vitamins that will straighten me out before I go on vacation, two weeks from now?"

The factor of time is part of the nutrition equation. It takes time to get into trouble; it takes time (and effort) to reverse the process, and it is critically important that you understand this. Even more important is the fragility of the recovery: it may require five or ten years of poor nutrition to upset your estrogen equilibrium and six months of good nutrition to bring it back to normal—but if you stray from the path of good diet again, the penalties may show up in a few weeks. Earlier, I told you that the tissues have a memory of insults. They do, and this you must remember.

It is useful, too, for you to understand the steps by which you arrive at the effects of an imbalanced diet, for this sequence will emphasize how a "well nourished" woman can be the victim of a diet which is allowing excess amounts of female hormone to assault the integrity of her body. The first stage in nutritional deficiency is failure of supply. Most frequently, this means a poor diet, but it can also be caused by food factors which interfere with the utilization of a nutrient, or even destroy it. An example is a substance in raw fish which destroys Vitamin B_1. It raised havoc with minks, but since they have a cash value, the problem was immediately researched and solved. An everyday example is the tannin in tea, which complexes with thiamin (B_1), converting the vitamin into a "bound" form which the body is unable to break down and utilize. This effect is demonstrable in as little as two weeks of excessive tea consumption. It is, of course, possible that the nutrient is adequately supplied and is in an absorbable form, but the absorption or utilization is impaired.

After failure of supply, blood levels of the factor begin to drop, but the body intervenes, and in an effort to eke out and more equitably distribute the nutrient, the blood borrows from the tissue supplies. When these reserves are depleted, as a last-ditch measure, the organ reserves are used.

If you, as proprietor and tenant of all this marvelous, self-protecting chemical machinery, don't do something about the problem—which, not recognizing it, you're unlikely to do—the next stage is interference with the function of the body. This can take shape as any of a hundred symptoms. They not only don't suggest poor nutrition as a cause, but are likely to be tagged as "psychosomatic," for the good reason that a "complete physical examination," not specifically aimed at nutritional status, shows nothing wrong—another way of saying that the examination won't find what it's not seeking. Among your symptoms at this stage could be headache, irritability, unprovoked weeping, anxiety, insomnia, unrefreshing sleep (waking up more tired than you were when you went to bed), loss of appetite, poor muscle tone, poor elimination, fatigability, or blurring of vision which isn't improved by eyeglasses. Others include heightened premenstrual tension, menstrual cramps, breast cysts, and other characteristics of the "normal, well-nourished American woman." At this stage, she is more accurately described as a helpless target for excessive estrogen activity, released by her liver, which is normal on conventional medical tests, but incapable of maintaining its nutritionally dependent control of the female hormone.

If the disturbances in function aren't recognized for what they are—and the odds are that they won't be, unless you are in the hands of a competent medical nutritionist—the next stage in the development of a nutritional deficiency will be microscopic changes in the tissues. These, too, will go undetected, since both you and your practitioner will take a dim view of having razor-thin biopsies of your organs submitted to examination under the microscope.

Finally, there will appear macroscopic changes in tissues, visible to the naked eye. These might include a beefy-red tongue, shiny and bare, and cracks at the corners of the mouth; fragility of the small blood vessels, apparent in a tendency to easy bruising, or bleeding of the gums; changes in the texture and manageability of your hair, coarsening of your skin, and weakening of your nails . . . Now the science of medicine will, at long last, grant that you are the victim of an inadequate diet, unless you should happen to fall into the hands of a psychoanalytically oriented practitioner, who will promptly blame the whole mess on your mother's domineering techniques of toilet training.

In what you have just read, there are conclusions of great importance to you. It is obvious that time is a factor in the development of nutritional deficiencies, exactly as it is in recovery from them. It may take you years to arrive at the penalties of a poor diet, and it may take months for us to reverse them with a good diet. If you remember my earlier remark about the tissues having a memory of insults, you will realize that undoing the benefits of that nutritional recovery will take even less time.

Though your poor diet may have allowed estrogen to begin its insidious attack on the integrity of the body, there may be no overt, clearly recognizable symptoms of nutritional deficiency, at least not as they are listed in the medical texts which most physicians studied. The *classic* symptoms of deficiency—beriberi, pellagra, and scurvy—are what your doctors never see, and it is on that basis that they consider you to be well fed.

So is it possible for you to be a "well-nourished" female by current medical standards, and still be a victim of deficiencies which begin their attack by initiating premenstrual and menstrual disturbances and, possibly, breast cysts, and then ultimately pave the way to estrogen-dependent cancer.

In a sense, then, this book sets up the proposition that the "well-nourished" female can be *cured*. To accomplish that, you *must* change your dietary habits, and you *must* learn to use food supplements properly. There is no royal road, there are no magic pills with overnight effects, but the short-term dividends—normalization of the menstrual cycle, improved health, appearance, and vitality—are alone worth the effort, and the ultimate goal—control of the female hormone to mitigate its potential for lethal mischief—how do we set a price on that?

Even if you accept these basic premises, you are not to be persuaded easily that your menus represent an unprecedented journey into the unknown, with unpredictable results. Would a deep-sea fish be likely to discover salt water? Here are three observations, taken from major newspapers, which may give you a useful overview:

1. A research center fed average American meals to rhesus monkeys, to study the early development of atherosclerosis (hardening of the arteries). None of the animals fed from an average American market basket lived long enough to develop the disease.
2. The U.S. Department of Agriculture publishes monographs on human nutrition, one of which flatly states that up to 90 percent of our sicknesses could be alleviated or prevented by simple changes in our eating habits.
3. A veterinarian was called to an affluent home to attend a sick puppy. He was struck by the contrast between the sicknesses and debilitation of the pedigreed animal and the glowing health of its owner, a little boy. He later discovered that the child was giving the dog *his* breakfast cereal, and he himself was eating the dog food.

How do you drift into a way of eating which sickens and kills animals, and crowds our hospitals and medical facilities? You begin by assuming that the average is normal. What is more American than apple pie? There is *nothing* normal about a dessert which in one portion supplies 12 teaspoonfuls of sugar—unless you take it a la mode, which brings the sugar total up to *18* teaspoonfuls per portion. (Keep in mind that I have repeatedly observed reduced premenstrual tension and shortening of menstruation from nothing more than reduction of sugar intake.) In nature, finding *anything* that will give you 18 teaspoonfuls of sugar per portion is difficult, and eating it would be more so. Would you eat twenty apples at one sitting? But you'll consume the sugar of twenty apples in pie or soda pop—and come back for more. In response to that accusation, I receive three arguments from women:

1. I don't eat very much sugar—in fact, rarely use it. I watch my weight.
2. I do use sugar, but moderately.
3. I can't help myself—I have a craving for sweets.

To the first two groups, there is a simple answer. Most of the sugar you consume isn't visible until it surfaces on your hips, disturbs your pancreas and places you on the road toward diabetes or hypoglycemia, or buys your dentist another annuity. Sugar comes to you in foods you don't think contain it, and in forms you don't recognize as sugar.

(Before I explain that, it's pertinent to note that all the vitamins that should be in sugar are removed. One of these is Vitamin B_6, and you learned in Chapter 4 that this vitamin is very effective in reducing water retention in the premenstrual week. It is also related to the chemistry of estrogenic hormone. Eating large amounts of sugar increases the Vitamin B_6 deficiency which high levels of female hormone can cause.)

The sugar taken from the bowl for use in coffee and other beverages is but the tip of the sweet iceberg. Sugar is used on breakfast cereal, and the cereal already has sugar as one of its ingredients. Ketchup contains a large amount of sugar. The cheesecake you think is a protein dessert has a high sugar content. There is even sugar added to some brands of salt—watch for the word *dextrose* on the label. And, speaking of labels, the manufacturers of processed foods manage neatly to disguise the amount of sugar in their products, by listing sugars according to their sources. Thus the label will name sugar, corn syrup solids, and glucose. If they were totaled, sugar would be the dominating ingredient in some products, and would have to be the first ingredient given on the label. Broken into three categories, sugar appears to be a minor ingredient. Why this deception isn't eliminated by the government is a good question.

There is sugar in canned green peas, in bottled salad dressing, in baked products—including all types of bread. There is sugar in the coating of your vitamin pills, and more sugar in the antacid tablet you take to relieve the indigestion you developed from eating too much sugar. When we finish this discussion, I am providing a table which lists sources of sugar in the diet. Do study it, and avoid the foods listed as containing inordinate amounts of this overused sweetening agent, or minimize their use.

Inevitably, as a nutritionist who has evoked every question Americans can think of—and some they never did—I can anticipate most of the question marks raised by these remarks about sugar. What about brown sugar? What about turbinado or raw sugar? And what about honey? The answer is, there is *no* form of sugar which at the present American level of intake is good for you. Dark brown, raw, and turbinado sugar do contain a little chromium, which helps (and is, indeed, necessary to) sugar metabolism, but all forms of sugar raise vitamin need and depress the supply, and all forms cause disturbances of blood chemistry. According to my friend, Professor John Yudkin of Queen Elizabeth College, University of London, these disturbances include raising of blood triglycerides, fasting insulin (in blood taken from a patient who has not eaten), corticosteroids, stomach hydrochloric acid, and blood cholesterol levels; enlarging the liver, shrinking the pancreas, and enlarging the adrenal glands; and topping all these off by increasing the adhesiveness of blood platelets. It all adds up to increasing the risk of diabetes, hypoglycemia, heart attacks, strokes, and stomach ulcers. The mischief-making factor in sugar is fructose—and honey is an excellent source of fructose.

All this brings you face-to-face with a resigned acceptance of the fact that you *must* reduce sugar to the status of a condiment. You don't use salt and pepper by the pound; why do you accept recipes which begin with "Take 2 cups of sugar"? Consider this observation, living as you do in a country where 80 percent of all adults over the age of thirty-five have periodontal disease: loose teeth are the threat that most commonly leads to dentures; a diet free of sugar has been shown to tighten loose teeth measurably in less than two weeks!

Now look at the amount of sugar concealed in foods where you (1) didn't suspect its presence or (2) didn't realize the quantity present:

Distribution of Sugar in Common Foods

(100 grams = 20 teaspoonfuls = 3½ ounces = 400 calories)

Food	*Amount*	*Serving*	*Sugar Equivalent*
Candy:			
Hershey bar	60 gm.	1 (25¢ size)	7 tsp. sugar
Chocolate cream	13 gm.	1 (35 to lb.)	2 tsp. sugar
Chocolate fudge	30 gm.	1½ in. sq. (15 to 1 lb.)	4 tsp. sugar
Chewing gum		1 stick	⅓ tsp. sugar
Lifesaver		1 usual size	⅓ tsp. sugar
Cake:			
Chocolate cake	100 gm.	2-layer, icing (1/12 cake)	15 tsp. sugar
Angel cake	45 gm.	1 pc. (1/12 large cake)	6 tsp. sugar
Sponge cake	50 gm.	1/10 of average cake	6 tsp. sugar
Cream puff (iced)	80 gm.	1 average, custard-filled	5 tsp. sugar
Doughnut (plain)	40 gm.	3 in. in diameter	4 tsp. sugar
Cookies:			
Macaroons	25 gm.	1 large or 2 small	3 tsp. sugar
Gingersnaps	6 gm.	1 medium	1 tsp. sugar
Brownies	20 gm.	2×2×¾ in.	3 tsp. sugar
Custards:			
Custard, baked		½ cup	4 tsp. sugar
Gelatin		½ cup	4 tsp. sugar
Junket		⅛ qt.	3 tsp. sugar

Food	*Amount*	*Serving*	*Sugar Equivalent*
Ice cream:			
Ice cream		⅛ qt.	5 to 6 tsp. sugar
Sherbet		⅛ qt.	6 to 8 tsp. sugar
Pie:			
Apple pie		1/6 medium pie	12 tsp. sugar
Cherry pie		1/6 medium pie	14 tsp. sugar
Custard, coconut pie		1/6 medium pie	10 tsp. sugar
Pumpkin pie		1/6 medium pie	10 tsp. sugar
Sauce:			
Chocolate sauce	30 gm.	1 heaping tsp., thick	4½ tsp. sugar
Marshmallow	7.6 gm.	1 (60 to 1 lb.)	1½ tsp. sugar
Spreads:			
Jam	20 gm.	1 Tbs. level or 1 heaping tsp.	3 tsp. sugar
Jelly	20 gm.	1 Tbs. level or 1 heaping tsp.	2½ tsp. sugar
Marmalade	20 gm.	1 Tbs. level or 1 heaping tsp.	3 tsp. sugar
Honey	20 gm.	1 Tbs. level or 1 heaping tsp.	3 tsp. sugar
Milk drinks:			
Chocolate (all milk)		1 cup, 5 oz. milk	6 tsp. sugar
Cocoa (all milk)		1 cup, 5 oz. milk	4 tsp. sugar
Cocomalt (all milk)		1 glass, 8 oz. milk	4 tsp. sugar

Soft drinks:			
Coca Cola	180 gm.	1 bottle, 6 oz.	4⅓ tsp. sugar
Ginger ale	180 gm.	6-oz. glass	4⅓ tsp. sugar
Cooked fruits:			
Peaches, canned in syrup	10 gm.	2 halves, 1 Tbs. juice	3½ tsp. sugar
Rhubarb, stewed	100 gm.	½ cup, sweetened	8 tsp. sugar
Applesauce (no sugar)	100 gm.	½ cup, scant	2 tsp. sugar
Prunes, stewed, sweetened	100 gm.	4 to 5 medium 2 Tbs. juice	8 tsp. sugar
Dried fruits:			
Apricots, dried	30 gm.	4 to 6 halves	4 tsp. sugar
Prunes, dried	30 gm.	3 to 4 medium	4 tsp. sugar
Dates, dried	30 gm.	3 to 4, stoned	4½ tsp. sugar
Figs, dried	30 gm.	1½ to 2 small	4 tsp. sugar
Raisins	30 gm.	¼ cup	4 tsp. sugar
Fruits and fruit juices:			
Fruit cocktail	120 gm.	½ cup, scant	5 tsp. sugar
Orange juice	100 gm.	½ cup, scant	2 tsp. sugar
Pineapple juice, unsweetened	100 gm.	½ cup, scant	$2^3/_5$ tsp. sugar
Grapefruit juice, unsweetened	100 gm.	½ cup, scant	$2^1/_5$ tsp. sugar
Grape juice, commercial	100 gm.	½ cup, scant	3⅔ tsp. sugar

Now that we have coped with the arguments of those who believe they use no sugar or very little, let's take care of the woman who frankly confesses a sweet tooth. If her craving for sugar is really compulsive, she is more deserving of sympathy than you might suppose, because she may be a victim of an unrecognized allergy. I know that it will seem strange that you can be addicted to a food because you're allergic to it, but there is a reasonable explanation for the phenomenon.

To explain as simply as possible: the first reaction to eating something to which you are allergic is a stimulation of the nervous system—a "high," in the language of drug users. (That's why a rise in the pulse rate is a test for allergy.) That high, which is pleasant (whether or not you're *consciously* aware of it), gradually fades, and is succeeded by the unpleasant allergic reaction, whatever that may be, which depends not only on the nature of the food, but on your personal chemistry. It might be an allergic headache, or irritability, or nervousness, or blurring of vision, or drowsiness—whatever your Achilles' heel dictates. If, however, you take another portion of the offending food, it renews the stimulation and delays the severe allergic reaction. In this way, you become addicted to the foods to which you are allergic. When this kind of chemistry is operating, it is easy to demonstrate that the food addiction is in fact allergic in origin, for patients with an obsessive craving for cane sugar may *not* crave beet sugar—which is to say they aren't allergic to sugar, but to its source.

Neuroallergists who solve such problems may conquer the addictive use of sugar in one of two ways:

1. A great dilution of the offending food, in this case sugar, will neutralize the allergic reaction, and may help to control the sweet tooth.

2. High doses of Vitamin B_6 and Vitamin C, as much as one gram (1,000 milligrams) of each, frequently are effective in overcoming the craving for sweets, which really means they have an effective action against allergy. It's interesting to realize that if you were consuming sugar-cane, instead of the sugar extracted from it, you'd be supplied with Vitamin B_6; and if you were using fruits as a modest source of sugar, you'd automatically be supplied with Vitamin C. Nature proposes, man disposes.

Reducing your sugar intake calls for nothing more than a sense of discretion. Why buy canned fruit in heavy syrup if light-syrup pack is available? And what's the matter with water-packed fruit, even if it's labeled for diabetics? You don't have to wait for diabetes, you know. You don't have to buy presweetened cereals, some of which, unfortunately including those labeled "natural," contain as much as 40 percent sugar. If you taste your tea, coffee, or other beverages before sweetening them, you will not feel the need for your usual amount of sweetening. If you bake at home, strive for a tart apple pie: it's certainly a more gourmet selection than one so sweet that the apples can't be tasted. If you must eat cake, avoid the icing; and if you bake at home, try reducing the sugar content of your own cakes. Since sugar contributes to texture as well as to flavor, you will find a lower limit below which you can't go—but that loss of sugar is a gain for liver function. Let me spell that out: sugar requires B vitamins to "burn" it in the body. Thus it increases the need and diminishes the supply. And those B vitamins, as you surely now know, are critically important to you, as a woman. In fact, I've long thought that adoption of the American sweet tooth by Japanese women is one of the changes in their food habits which vitiate their resistance to breast cancer.

The riposte to this discussion is predictable: what about the artificial sweeteners? Philosophically, I must reject them; I'm trying to reeducate your palate, which isn't going to eventuate by the substitution of an artificial sweetener for an artificially concentrated natural one. In addition, there are unanswered questions about the safety of saccharin. If you must use it, stop every third week and let the body rid itself of the chemical. And if you're even possibly pregnant, don't use saccharin at all.

Your problem with sugar is but a facet of the failure of the American woman's diet to support optimal liver function. Knowing now what you do about the importance of the Vitamin B Complex to you, how do you react when I tell you that this entire group of vitamins is removed in the processing of the sugar, cereals, grains, and flour which make up 50 percent of your entire calorie intake—half of your food, in essence? And that isn't all: in the manufacture of white flour from wheat, seventeen nutrients are significantly depleted. Three of these are restored in "enrichment" of flour and bread. Two of those restored are those *rats* need to break down female hormone. Among the unrestored are those *you* need for that purpose.

Where do the others go? Into pig feed—as a result of which, the animals' diet, largely based on by-products of flour milling, shows these superiorities to white flour, as appraised by Dr. Henry Schroeder, Dartmouth College's expert on minerals:

21 times the Vitamin B_1 (thiamin)
14 times the Vitamin B_2 (riboflavin)
16 times the niacin (B_3)
14 times the Vitamin B_6 (pyridoxin)*
4 times the pantothenic acid
11 times the folic acid
17 times the Vitamin E (tocopherols)*
2 times the choline*
7 times the calcium
9 times the phosphorus
12 times the magnesium
12 times the potassium
3 times the molybdenum

2 times the chromium*
14 times the manganese
6 times the iron
42 times the cobalt
12 times the zinc*

NOTE: Dr. Schroeder doesn't list inositol, but the pigs enjoy a higher intake of this factor, too. Both bran and wheat germ, among the millers' feeds for pigs, contain significant amounts of this nutrient.

The asterisk* that follows some of these vitamin-mineral listings is there to remind me to remind you that these are nutrients of particular importance to women. Other than choline and inositol, of which the importance to a woman was discussed earlier, the asterisked nutrients have actions which are also of great usefulness in preventing or treating disorders frequent in women. Vitamin B_6 is asterisked because, as I noted earlier, it reduces water retention in pregnancy and in the premenstrual week. Together with potassium, it is an effective treatment for hypertrophic arthritis. Together with zinc (which is asterisked for that reason) it may help to prevent or to control a type of schizophrenia not uncommon in women who must endure excessive stress. Among lesser but gratifying benefits, Vitamin B_6 and zinc may prevent stretch marks in pregnancy.

Chromium helps to regulate carbohydrate metabolism (the chemistry of starches and sugars in the body). This fact is peculiarly important to women, for high estrogen levels may trigger a latent diabetes—as the birth control pill, containing that hormone, is known to do. Inositol not only aids liver control of the female hormone, but studies of its action on the brain waves indicate that it acts like a natural tranquilizer, so much so that my good friend, Dr. Carl Pfeiffer, who has studied these electrical phenomena in the brain, calls inositol "the poor man's Valium." Unlike a drug, a vitamin may tranquilize, but it doesn't stifle creativity or make you vegetate. Vitamin E carries an asterisk because it dampens the transmission of anxiety from the emotional brain to the thinking brain, which for many women, in menopause and in the premenstrual week when the anxiety index often goes up, is a blessing. Considering the actions of nutrients removed from white flour and fed to animals, the industry can fairly be described as showering on hogs a level of good nutrition which women rarely achieve, yet need, in order to build resistance to breast and uterine cancer.

For decades, nutritionally sophisticated women have chosen whole-wheat bread, cereals, and flour, and thereby stopped the industry from casting these nutritional pearls before swine. When they have used white flour in baking, they have chosen unbleached flour, because the bleaching removes most of the little Vitamin E left after processing, and to it, they have added wheat germ. These practices—which earned for them the title of food faddists from AMA nutritionists, the nutritionally illiterate public and professions, and the white flour industry itself—are a classic example of the philosophy of *Catch 22.* In essence, these "food faddists" are retaining in or restoring to the diet the important nutrients the millers prefer to sell as pig feed. Consider the nutrient values of wheat germ, which is to wheat what the egg yolk is to the egg: the source of new life, and as such, a storehouse of good nutrition. Wheat germ supplies significant amounts of thiamin (B_{10}), riboflavin (B_2), niacin (B_3), *pyridoxin* (B_6), tocopherols (E), protein, unsaturated fat, *inositol, choline,* fiber, iron, magnesium, and phosphorus.

Like all good foods, wheat germ spoils quickly. (When a food doesn't spoil, throw it out; when it does, eat it while it's fresh.) Buy wheat germ, and be sure it's not defatted, for with the fat, the Vitamin E departs, and that, you will remember, may protect not only against malignancy, but also against premature aging. Always buy wheat germ in vacuum-packed containers which, once opened, should be stored in the refrigerator, with the lid on.

Bran supplies the same nutrients, its content of Vitamin B_6 and zinc being high, its inositol and choline values useful, and its fiber content really indispensable. Fiber is another of the dietary factors of which you are deprived as a result of our biologically insane techniques of grain processing. As a result, you are unnecessarily exposed to the risk of appendicitis, diverticulosis, diverticulitis, varicose veins, rectal polyps and hemorrhoids, and bowel cancer, to mention only a few of the disorders of the digestive tract and blood vessels which are common among us, but rare in primitives on a high-fiber diet—until they are seduced by our supermarket foods.

The first step in helping liver function, then, is to bring whole-grain values back to the diet by the use of wheat germ and bran. Bran is easily incorporated in other foods, ranging from bran muffins to the addition of bran to other cereals, dry and cooked. (It is also available in tablet form, for the gulp and gallop set.) Bran combines well with yogurt, too, but that good food must be bought with discretion, for there are brands with more calories from sugar than from the milk, which is true of the varieties containing fruit and of those flavored with vanilla and chocolate. Buy plain yogurt, or, better, make your own. If you need guidance and recipes for the use of bran, there are a number of cookbooks and other texts you can consult, including my own cookbook, and those by Beatrice Trum Hunter and Adelle Davis.

Wheat germ can be combined with other cereals, or used as one; it is probably the best dry cereal on the market. When you bake, add a teaspoon of wheat germ to each cup of flour, as a basic recipe which will not alter the characteristics of your accustomed baked products. The amount can be increased, but the sky is not the limit; too much wheat germ is like adding too many eggs to bread or cake, culminating in a product so heavy that strongmen will be needed to convey it to the table.

If you use whole grains routinely, you will, of course, bring home the germ and bran of the grain, sans extra charge. This means whole wheat in place of white flour products, brown rice in place of white, whole barley to replace pearled barley, whole buckwheat, whole rye, and cornmeal which has not been degerminated. In other words, you will have decided that you prefer to have the Vitamin B Complex, the Vitamin E, and the trace minerals in your grains, rather than having them diverted to animal feedstuffs. If sugar intake is not reduced, your fiber intake will *not* reach adequacy merely because you are eating whole grains. Extra bran and fiber from fruits and vegetables will be necessary to offset the loss of fiber from sugar processing—which is significant. (We make wallboard and acoustic paneling from this fiber—and develop lethal disease for lack of it.) Bran cereals (if not high in sugar) or bran tablets will repair the deficit.

From long experience, I know that the preceding admonition will raise a host of questions about bread. For example, what about rye bread? Commercial rye bread is equivalent to commercial white bread; in fact, it contains as much overprocessed wheat flour as it does overprocessed rye flour. Pumpernickel? This is fermented rye bread, colored with burned sugar. Look for the term "caramel color" on the label, and you will know what to avoid. Look for a whole-wheat bread made with stone-ground flour. If you can't find it in your supermarket, you will find it at the health food store, along with other whole-grain cereals, breads, crackers, and flours. While you're buying whole grains at the health food store, let's learn to buy and use desiccated liver and brewer's yeast, for it isn't a matter of choosing brands at random.

Desiccated (which means dried) liver tablets are marketed by many companies. Two processes of drying the organ meat are used: vacuum drying and solvent extraction. The vacuum-dried is technically a better product, for the reason that the fat-soluble nutrients of liver are retained, whereas the solvent will inevitably remove them. Argentine liver is a preferable source, because the animals raised on the pampas are not subjected to insecticide sprays, and they aren't dosed with diethylstilbestrol, which is synthetic female hormone. (Your liver, properly fed, will break down this form of estrogen, too, but it seems illogical to bring more estrogen into the body, does it not?) In buying liver tablets or capsules, then, seek a brand—there are a number—made from Argentine livers, and dried by the vacuum process. Dose? There is no "dose"—this is food, not medication. You take a handful daily. Some people take thirty a day. The nutritionally sophisticated will wonder about the cholesterol content of liver. I don't want to burden the average reader with still more technical details, so suffice it to say that only those who have a medically recognized problem in metabolizing cholesterol need be concerned about a generous intake. Two thirds of the cholesterol in the body is made there—and the synthesis increases if you reduce the dietary intake, because cholesterol happens to be essential to life. The low-cholesterol fad will one day be remembered as another of the transient crazes which periodically sweep the professions and the public.

Most of the brewer's yeast on the market is labeled "primary yeast." The term is used to differentiate between this type of yeast, which is grown for use as a supplement, and the older type, which was first used to ferment alcoholic beverages and then, spent, sold for use as a dietary supplement. Since this use was "secondary," the supplement manufacturers use the term *primary* to let you know that the product was specifically grown to be used as a supplement to the human diet. The point isn't academic, for yeast used for brewing may be low in vitamins, the brewer being interested only in fermenting action, whereas the supplement manufacturer will pick types of yeast with much more value in essential nutrients.

The yeasts differ widely in odor, taste, and solubility. Some brands are not only more nutritious, but are much more palatable, and it pays to buy a few brands—selected on the basis of the vitamin-mineral-protein assay on the label—and stay with the one you find pleases your palate. Do examine the label statements of potencies carefully. Some brands contain Vitamin B_{12}, for example, naturally occurring from raising the yeast on buttermilk whey or another culture media reinforced with the vitamin; and some do not. Some have higher values in Vitamin B_6, pantothenic acid, or other factors. Protein value may start in the 40s and go up to 50 percent protein or even higher. These factors combine to determine whether a given product is worth more to you. You may buy the yeast in powder, capsule, or tablet form. The powders blend well with peanut butter; some people use them on cereals, others take them in tomato juice, and they are often used in bread recipes and in meat loaf.

There is a type of yeast which is less desirable. This is "torula" yeast, which is a totally different strain, often grown on the waste liquors from paper manufacture. It doesn't contain selenium, which you have learned is an important trace nutrient for you. If the product doesn't tell you which kind of yeast it represents, don't buy it. Makers of good products have nothing to hide.

The question of dose again is raised. I encounter women who take two tablets of brewer's yeast daily, and feel nutritionally virtuous. When I talk with them, I am always reminded of the pioneering research of Dr. Tom Spies, one of the greats in the field of medical nutrition, who gave malnourished patients a high-protein, high-vitamin, high-mineral diet, complemented with multiple vitamins by mouth and by injection, plus *one quarter of a pound* of brewer's yeast and *one quarter of a pound* of desiccated liver daily. I am willing to make the assumption that you are not grossly malnourished, but two tablets—*one fifteenth of an ounce daily?* A significant amount would be one or two tablespoons of brewer's yeast each day, always with a meal—you don't take supplements without food. In one-gram tablets, this would be from fifteen to thirty tablets daily. Don't wrinkle your patrician, if undernourished, nose. The goals of this nutritional program being what they are, the schedule is a lot less trouble than the penalties for eating improperly.

Since millions of us are allergic—for which, in the main, we are indebted to the substitution of cow's milk formulae for breastfeeding—I must anticipate plaintive complaints from those allergic to liver, and those who derive from brewer's yeast a complex of intestinal upsets, ranging from too much laxative action (for which some women are grateful) to gas or indigestion. If you can't, you can't. The program will lead to its goal if supported by a proper diet and a Vitamin B Complex concentrate with an adequate formula. The yeast and the dried liver will speed the response, and yield certain benefits from the unknown factors of the Vitamin B Complex—but again, if you can't tolerate them, our goal can still be achieved.

There is a virtual explosion of Vitamin B Complex brands in the health food stores—more so than in the pharmacies. Unless you keep your needs clearly in mind, the profusion of these products will confuse you. Most of these supplements supply meaningful potencies of thiamin, riboflavin, and niacin. Some of them go overboard on these three vitamins, but such potencies as 50 milligrams of each are wasteful and expensive, except for those who have a real problem in poor utilization of the vitamins or inadequate resistance to stress.

In view of the interaction of folic acid and para-aminobenzoic acid (PABA) with estrogen, many B Complex supplements provide more of these nutrients than I would approve. From 200 to 400 micrograms of folic acid and up to 30 milligrams of PABA will be acceptable, not more—and I'd prefer about half those amounts.

A majority of the concentrates don't contain enough choline and inositol, because of lack of demand for these vitamins, as I told you earlier, and because of their bulk as compared to a tablet or capsule of a size which can easily be swallowed. Some of them don't supply enough pyridoxin (B_6) to meet a woman's needs. My specifications call for a daily intake of 1,000 milligrams of choline (1 gram), which may be offered as choline chloride, dihydrogen citrate, or other form; 500 milligrams (½ gram) of inositol; and at least 25 milligrams of pyridoxin (B_6) daily.

If you can't find a brand of Vitamin B Complex supplement which meets these standards in these three factors, there is still no real difficulty, for all three vitamins are available separately, in tablet, or capsule form. There are, in fact, supplements which combine inositol and choline, sometimes with added methionine, which is a protein (amino) acid which is also helpful to liver function. Before you surrender to the necessity of using separate supplements to bring up the intake of choline, inositol, and Vitamin B_6, read the B Complex labels carefully. You may find brands where doubling the recommended dose—say, of one tablet daily—will provide the requisite amount of these factors, without raising the levels of the others to astronomical (though harmless) and expensive amounts.

Your next quest is a multiple vitamin–mineral supplement, some of which are available in a dosage of a single tablet daily. This supplies factors which are not incorporated in the Vitamin B Complex concentrate, as well as some which are. The added nutrients may (and should) include iodine, Vitamin E, and Vitamin C—all important vitamins to you—plus calcium. The added calcium is important, particularly if you don't use milk and cheese in significant amounts.

Many women unnecessarily become victims of osteoporosis, a weakening of the bones which often follows menopause, and the disorder, which is painful, sometimes crippling, often a prelude to fractures, is less frequent in those who have a lifetime generous intake of calcium. The mineral also offsets a tendency of a form of inositol to raise calcium needs.

In the health food store, as in the supermarket and pharmacy, avoid the products which contain preservatives and coal-tar dyes. These are gratuitous hazards. The cosmetic appeal is unnecessary, and competently formulated supplements will have an adequate shelf life without BHT, BHA, and other petroleum-based preservatives. You can generally identify the undesirably dyed products, because brilliant reds, purples, and yellows are invariably triumphs of cosmetic chemistry over nature. The presence of preservatives will be indicated on the label, and don't discount the possibility of their use even by manufacturers of products supposed to be healthful. I recently encountered a "chewable" vitamin for children which contains BHT, BHA (originally formulated to keep the colors in motion-picture film from fading), coal-tar dyes, and saccharin! Such a chemical cocktail, given to a hyperactive child, might perpetuate (and even increase) his problems.

Thus far, in enriching your diet with the Vitamin B Complex, we have discussed desiccated liver, brewer's yeast, a concentrate of the Vitamin B Complex, the use of wheat germ and bran in your recipes, and discarding processed carbohydrates, such as white flour, white sugar, and white rice. Additional sources of the Vitamin B Complex which are often neglected are the organ meats, such as liver, and also kidneys, sweetbreads, and brains.* These have already been described as the body's safe-deposit vaults for

*When dietary levels of selenium are high, breast cancer rates are low. Kidney tissue has about sixteen times the selenium value of muscle meats; liver has four times the value.

storage of critical nutrients, on which the blood and other tissues draw in times of need. They are neglected treasures, for the American housewife concentrates her meat-buying selection on muscles: steaks, chops, and roasts. The laws of economics operate and, since she is bidding against her neighbor for a finite supply of muscle meats, their prices soar while, for want of demand, those of the organ meats, the best nutrition in the animal, drop. It is true that liver is suspect because of the use of diethylstilbestrol in fattening cattle, but ultimately, that will be banned. In the interim, buy liver which is "organic"—meaning that the animal was not subjected to such hormonal manipulation—and do buy the other organ meats. Incidentally, the least prized forms of liver have the most nutrition: calf liver has the least, the animal not having lived long enough to enrich its reserves. Pork liver and lamb liver are better food, and beef liver is an excellent buy. Chicken liver is intermediate in value, but still an excellent food.

We have reached one of several points in this book at which I must cope with not the possibility, but the probability, that some of you can't tolerate whole-wheat bread, find wheat germ or bran less than friendly, or are allergic to liver or sensitive to yeast. Having written an entire text on satisfying individual differences in nutritional needs and tolerances *(Look Younger, Feel Healthier,* also published by Grosset & Dunlap), I am certainly sensitively aware that Mrs. Jack Spratt does exist, and has her dietary problems. That, in fact, is one of the reasons for the use of the vitamin supplements, not only to meet needs increased by prior deficiency, but as a kind of diet insurance which compensates for losses in cooking and processing and for differences in tolerance for good foods.

You needn't think, then, that you're going to escape the nutritionist by announcing that whole-wheat bread makes you break out in cupcakes, for there is a recipe for a type of white bread which gives you whole-grain values, and is very often tolerated by those who can't adapt to the roughage of whole grains. The recipe was devised by an old friend and fine nutritionist, Dr. Clive McKay of Cornell University, and is known, appropriately, as the Cornell formula. You'll find it in the Appendix. If you bake at home, this recipe will be both a treat and a nutritional dividend for you and the family.

7

Taking the "Die" out of "Diet"

We have two problems: I have you; you have me. Years of educating women in nutrition have indelibly taught me that for your sex, calories may be a greater concern than disease. Don't challenge me, for I can prove it. As an example, to obtain the iron you need and to replace that which you lose in menstruals prolonged by poor diet, I say you must eat about 3,000 calories daily, from food well enough selected to yield 18 milligrams of iron daily. You will immediately protest that you can't eat more than 2,000 calories without gaining weight, and given a choice between glamorous anemia and obesity with high hemoglobin, you know very well how your vote will go. Common sense rarely influences dietary habits—because they *are* habits. I've seen diabetics cheat with forbidden foods, impassively ignoring their doctors' warnings of penalties ranging from cataracts to coma. I've watched hypoglycemics yield to the craving for sweets, though quite aware that sugar pushes them into neurotic behavior, anxiety, suicidal depression, epileptiform convulsions, impotence, or frigidity. I remember how Whipple's patients reacted when they were told that that great physician had discovered that eating raw liver twice daily would rescue them from the inexorable, deadly progress of pernicious anemia. They chose death, instead. I've been told that famine-ridden people of the East have been known to elect starvation, rather than eat the unaccustomed wheat we indefatigably ship to them. But you *are* reading this book, and I must assume that you're in a teachable frame of mind, and ready to act on a lifetime menu framework—not a *diet*, because that is something you eventually stop—a plan which will bring you as close to optimal nutrition (and heightened resistance to cancer) as the state of the art will permit.

Rigid dietary habits fade when cancer strikes. I've seen the extremes in nutrition to which desperate women resort—the consumption of gallons of vegetable juices, of pancreatic enzymes, of apricot pits, of asparagus by the pound—an understandable grasping at folklore which might shut the door to death. Rarely, they succeed, but I still prefer the way of prevention, for miracle cures are more than passingly infrequent. Let me tell you of two happy people whose story will emphasize the urgency of the message in this book.

Leaving the nutrition class I was teaching at the New York Institute of Technology one bitter cold night in late winter, I found a professional man and his wife waiting for me, both of them in tears. The practitioner explained that a Pap smear had revealed advanced precancerous changes in his wife's tissues, and some evidence of early cancer. Could I, he pleaded, refer him to a physician willing to try therapies other than the conventional surgery, irradiation, and chemotherapy, in which he had little faith? Making no promises, I did so, referring him to Dr. Andrew Ivy, the brilliant physiologist who was then deep in research with a new and promising treatment for cancer. I suggested, though, that while a better-fed patient should respond better to a treatment aimed, as Ivy's was, at stimulating the body's own immunological defenses, the fact was that no attention was paid to the diet as part of this therapy. I recommended that the doctor, while waiting for the desired appointment, use the time to good advantage by improving his wife's nutrition. I gave him several of my books to supply the type of guidance in selection of foods and supplements which you will derive from this chapter.

A semester later they returned, bursting to tell me of their happiness. A recent Pap smear showed no abnormalities, and her last examination had been "essentially negative." I surmised that Dr. Ivy must also have been delighted, but the professional man shook his head. "I couldn't get an appointment," he said, "it would have taken too long. All I did was to change her diet, and supplement it intensively."

I heard this in empathy and with wryness, knowing that a single case proves nothing. Yet he had monitored her progress with frequent Pap smears, and was distressed when I commented that I'd never tell the story before any scientific assemblage. Which I didn't, but it's almost ten years since that conversation on that cold night, and she faithfully follows the pattern of nutrition that keeps estrogen activity down—and she remains well. The establishment would call this a spontaneous remission, but under whatever title, the history is a fitting preface to the information I am about to give you, which provides the guidelines for the level of good nutrition that pays dividends in prevention. Such nutrition must be consistent, concentrated, and continuous—the three indispensable C's of optimal diet for maximum protection.

The amount of a vitamin needed for normal eyesight may be one fortieth of the intake needed for efficient reproduction. That is a more important statement than you may realize, for it means that a woman who must drastically change her diet when she becomes pregnant has really been eating improperly. It also means that menus that support motherhood, minus the extra calories the pregnant woman needs, will be those which, among many other benefits, will maintain the liver functions at highest efficiency. All this tells you why I am about to place you on menus with a provocative history. It is little realized that the first test of any nutritional program is its ability to support reproductive efficiency. It matters not what other benefits such a program may yield; if it doesn't perpetuate the breed, it is an exercise in futility. It is also little realized that the American menu fails miserably in meeting that challenge. We talk about a population explosion to demonstrate how fertile we are, but we don't count the childless couples trying to buy babies in the black market, nor do we hear the urgent voices of the women making the rounds of the fertility clinics and gynecologists' offices. Few of us, preoccupied with the population explosion, realize that 10 percent of our marriages are involuntarily barren and 16 percent of our young men incapable of fathering children, a percentage which rises with increasing age. Few know that about 5 percent of all births are premature and that approximately one conception in every four does not produce a living, healthy, normal baby. But, as demonstrated by successful conception of healthy infants in formerly infertile families, by highly successful support of pregnancies in thousands of women, and by reduction of the rate of prematurity by some 80 percent, the nutrition program in this chapter meets fully the challenge of supporting efficient reproduction, which constitutes the greatest of all nutritional demands in the life-span. And that is the kind of menu planning which will meet our objective of maximum encouragement for liver degradation of estrogenic hormone—which again isn't based on speculation, for it is from such menus and supplements that a great many women have earned the dividends of freedom from premenstrual and menstrual disturbances and cystic mastitis.

The daily intake should follow this food framework:

1 8-ounce glass of unstrained fruit juice. Citrus is preferable, and fresh-squeezed is superior to canned and frozen.

1 serving of fresh fruit, unpeeled. Wash thoroughly.

Two cups of cooked vegetables, choosing from as wide a variety as possible. Serve slightly undercooked.

1 cup of salad, using dark green leafy vegetables. Basic dressing should be additive-free pure vegetable oils, varied as much as possible, with such added seasonings as you prefer.

3 squares of butter.

1 serving of oatmeal, whole-wheat, or other whole-grain cereal, additive-free, with 1 teaspoonful of undefatted wheat germ. Pancakes or waffles from good recipes—not commercial mixes—may be substituted. Whole or nonfat milk, added as you choose. A teaspoon or two of coarse miller's bran in the cereal will help to keep elimination normal.

2 eggs daily, in any form—as such, or as part of eggnogs, baked dishes, custards, etc.

6 ounces of lean meat, fish, fowl, cheese, or any combination of these, with emphasis, in meat selections, on organs such as liver, kidney, tripe, sweetbreads.

4 slices of stone-ground whole-wheat, whole-rye, or whole-corn bread.

3 glasses of milk or equivalent in cheese, buttermilk, kefir, yogurt, or recipes in which milk is a significant ingredient. (Milk intolerance will be discussed later.)

DESSERTS: nutritious cookies (recipe provided later), whole gelatin, junket, custard, stewed or fresh fruit (with cheese, if preferred), fruit whip. No convenience desserts, no commercial cakes and cookies of the usual type. Some excellent cookies and cakes, whole-grain based, are available in health food stores. No ordinary commercial ice cream—it's 16 percent sugar, and may have excessive additive content. No whipped toppings—use real cream.

Do not use conventional spaghetti, macaroni, and noodles. In the health food stores and many supermarkets there are brands which are high in protein and starch-reduced. They are also more nutritious than ordinary varieties.

Within your calorie limitations, use nuts and seeds as snacks, for these are sources of new life, and filled with the nutrients needed to support it. If you're a snacker, these choices concentrate your good nutrition rather than dilute it as ordinary snacks do. And, speaking of nibbling: into how many meals you divide this food framework is your choice. There are those who feel and function better on frequent small meals, which do make easier control of weight, glucose metabolism, and blood cholesterol levels. There are those who simply can't eat more than two meals daily, and those who somehow function on one, though it's most difficult to achieve a balanced diet when it rests on just one leg. For the average person, the pattern of three meals daily is simply a concession to the schedules of the bus, job, or school, and has no relationship to the body's actual needs. You may be startled by your increased well-being when you increase the frequency and decrease the size of your meals.

Brewer's yeast, if you're not taking it as a supplement, may be added to appropriate recipes. So can wheat germ—in almost any recipe containing cereal or flour—and dried nonfat milk. If you're not familiar with the use of these high-nutrition additions to recipes in cooking and baking, consult the *Carlton Fredericks Cookbook for Good Nutrition* or the excellent cookbooks and baking guides by Beatrice

Trum Hunter and by Adelle Davis. Another excellent text is *Confessions of a Sneaky Cook* by Jane Kinderlehrer.

For the "I Can't Eat That!" Society

The impossible dream of the nutritionist is a cooperative public with uniform nutritional needs and tolerances, who can be neatly fitted into any dietary scheme that makes sense. The reality is a public hagridden by allergies which started when we began to feed babies on formulas, and which have now progressed to multiple sensitivities which seriously interfere with the health, function, and food selections of tens of millions of children and adults. If you add to these restrictions those based on food intolerances founded on heredity or idiosyncrasies, the only generalization permitted in nutrition is a broad statement of the inapplicability of generalizations. In the menu framework you have just read, there are a dozen possible impasses for the food-sensitive, including those with allergies or intolerances to whole grains, bran, wheat germ, milk, cheese, uncooked fruit, green salads, organ meats, or, for that matter, brewer's yeast. There will be some people—fortunately, a relatively small group—who won't be able to use some of the supplements which can compensate for necessary restrictions on food selection. The notes which follow will help those who must find alternates to some of the good foods.

If you and citrus fruits aren't compatible, use those fruits and juices you do find friendly. Tomato juice, though lower in Vitamin C than citrus, is a good food, and the deficit in ascorbic acid will be made up by the supplements. Apple juice, when fortified with added Vitamin C, is useful, though its high content of carbohydrate calories may be a negative consideration for those who function best on a low-carbohydrate diet. Pineapple juice supplies too much sugar to make calorie watchers happy.

If you are intolerant of vegetables in the raw—which

would include green salads—and some of the cooked vegetables also present a problem, pureed vegetables and the use of vegetable juices will partially compensate. Palatable vegetable juices can be prepared at home, inexpensively, with the proper juicer or blender.

If whole grains and your digestive tract will never be friends, you may achieve some of their essential values by fortifying processed cereals and unbleached white flour with wheat germ, starting with one teaspoonful per cup and gradually increasing when tolerance is established.

Milk disturbs many people. Allergy is the usual reason, but the adverse reaction may also be based on the lack of an enzyme needed to break down lactose (milk sugar). (It *is* allergy if hot milk before retiring makes you sleepy, or if your craving for milk becomes compulsive.) In many Jews, Blacks, and Orientals, diarrhea and flatulence produced by milk point to the missing enzyme, lack of which provides intestinal bacteria with milk sugar on which to work, with consequent disturbances of the colon. Sometimes, those with this problem can tolerate fermented milk products, such as yogurt, kefir, or acidophilus milk. Sometimes tolerance will permit one glass of milk daily, but not more. Occasionally, certified raw milk, which is still available from four dairies in the United States, will be better accepted than pasteurized. The converse is also true: some people who can't drink ordinary pasteurized milk are able to do so if the milk has been brought to a boil, then quickly chilled. The same phenomenon occurs with cheese. Those intolerant of naturally ripened cheeses made from pasteurized milk, which describes the average American product, may have less difficulty with cheeses from Switzerland, where the milk is not pasteurized and the processing temperature is well below that of the human body. In contrast is the American processed cheese, which not only originates with pasteurized milk, but is cooked to a uniform flavor; and this may increase tolerance. I believe that the point should now be clear that the heat applied—or not applied—to foods can make them more (or less) tolerable for a person with idiosyncratic reactions.

All this emphasis on dairy foods is based on two considerations which involve anticancer nutrition: their high-quality protein values, and their rich store of vitamins and minerals—particularly calcium, of which they are virtually an indispensable, concentrated source. If you can't consume them, your supplements, again, will protect you.

The menu framework you have just read was created with a reasonable consideration of the calorie ceiling which women must observe, but it obviously is not aimed at those who must lose weight. For that reason, another framework follows. It is a tested, highly successful, well-balanced reducing diet which is so arranged that you needn't count calories and you *can* stay within your diet even when dining away from home. Assuming that you're in normal health and your metabolism is normal—both highly generous assumptions on my part—this framework should melt away about two pounds per week, which is about as fast a weight loss as anyone should try to achieve. I know there are blitz diets which slim you faster. I also know that I've lost many good friends in the performing arts whose disasters with "wonder" diets have been attributed to complications after surgery, pneumonia, or overwork.

THE SANE WAY TO SLIMNESS

BREAKFAST

1 serving of fruit
1 egg or egg substitute
½ slice (thin) whole-wheat toast with ½ level tsp. butter
1 glass of skimmed milk
1 cup of coffee or tea (optional), with no sugar, cream, or milk

LUNCH

1 helping of lean meat, fish, fowl, or meat substitute
1 vegetable from Vegetable List A
1 salad (from Salad List)
1 serving of fruit or dessert
1 glass of skimmed milk or buttermilk
1 cup of coffee or tea (optional), with no sugar, cream, or milk

DINNER

1 cup of soup (optional)
1 helping of lean meat, fish, fowl, or meat substitute
2 vegetables from Vegetable List A and 1 from Vegetable List B

or

1 vegetable from Vegetable List A plus 1 from Vegetable List B plus 1 helping of salad (from Salad List)
1 portion of fruit or dessert
Coffee or tea (no sugar, cream, or milk)

Choose foods from the following lists:

SOUP LIST

Consommé
Clear vegetable soup
Beef broth
Mutton broth
Chicken broth
Other clear soups

NOTE: No creamed soups, none with milk or content of vegetables, meat, or cereals.

FRUIT LIST

Orange (1, small)
Grapefruit (½, medium size)
Apple (1, small)
Pineapple (2 average slices)
Peach (1)
Cantaloupe (½, medium size)
Melon (2-inch section of average-size melon)

Tangerine (1, large)
Berries (½ cup)
Apricots (2, medium size)
Grapes (12)
Cherries (10)
Pear (1, medium size)
Plums (2)
Nectarines (3)
Persimmon (½, small)
Fruit juices: 6 ounces (¾ water glass) grapefruit, orange (unsweetened)

MEAT LIST

Lean beefsteak (¼ lb., about 1 in. thick, 2½ in. square)
Roast beef (2 slices, about 3 in. square, ¼ in. thick)
Beef liver (1 slice, 3 in. square, ½ in. thick)
Beef tongue (2 average slices)
Beef kidney (¼ lb.)
Hamburger (¼ lb.)
Calf's liver (¼ lb.)
Lamb kidney (2, average size)
Lamb chop (1, about 2 in. square, ½ in. thick)
Roast lamb (1 slice, 3½ in. square, ¼ in. thick)
Mutton chop (2, medium size)
Boiled mutton (1 slice, 4 in. square, ½ in. thick)
Roast veal (1 slice, 3 in. by 2 in., ¼ in. thick)
Veal cutlet (1, average size)
Veal kidney (2, average size)
Chicken, white meat (2 slices, 4 in. square, cut very thin)
Chicken, broiler (½, medium size)
Chicken gizzards (2, average size)
Chicken, livers (2 whole, medium size)

FISH LIST

Sea bass (¼ lb.)
Bluefish (¼ lb.)
Cod, fresh (¼ lb. to ½ lb.)

Cod, salt (¼ lb. to ½ lb.)
Flounder (¼ lb. to ½ lb.)
Haddock (¼ lb. to ½ lb.)
Halibut (¼ lb.)
Kingfish (¼ lb.)
Pike (¼ lb.)
Porgy (¼ lb.)
Red snapper (¼ lb.)
Scallops (⅔ cup, raw measurement)
Shrimp (⅔ cup)
Smelt (¼ lb.)
Weakfish (¼ lb.)
Clams, round (10 to 12)
Crab meat (1 crab or ¾ cup flakes)
Lobster (½ small lobster or 1 cup flakes)
Mussels (4 large or 8 small)
Oysters (12 large)

MEAT SUBSTITUTES

Cottage cheese (⅔ cup)
Eggs (2)
Buttermilk (2 cups)
Whole milk (1 cup)
Skimmed milk (2 cups)

EGGS

Plain omelet
Poached
Soft-boiled
Hard-boiled
Raw

SUBSTITUTES FOR ONE EGG

Cottage cheese (4 Tbs.)
Lamb chop (1 small, lean)
Lamb kidney (1)
Calf's liver (2 oz.)
Mutton chop (1 small, lean)

Buttermilk (1 glass)
Skimmed milk (1 glass)

VEGETABLE LIST A

Asparagus (fresh or canned: 8)
String beans (½ cup)
Wax beans (½ cup)
Beet greens (2 heaping Tbs.)
Broccoli (1 5-in. stalk)
Brussels sprouts (½ cup)
Cabbage, cooked (½ cup)
Cabbage, raw (¾ cup, shredded)
Cauliflower (½ cup)
Celery (5 stalks)
Chard (½ cup)
Chicory (½ cup)
Eggplant (½ cup)
Endive (10 medium stalks)
Green pepper (1, medium size)
Kohlrabi (2 heaping Tbs.)
Leeks, chopped (⅓ cup)
Lettuce (10 leaves)
Radishes (5, medium size)
Sauerkraut (½ cup)
Spinach (½ cup)
Tomatoes, fresh (1)
Tomatoes, canned (½ cup)
Tomato juice: four ounces (½ cup)
Watercress (10 pieces)

VEGETABLE LIST B

Beets (2 heaping Tbs.)
Carrots (2 heaping Tbs.)
Chives (6)
Dandelion greens (3 heaping Tbs.)
Kale (2 heaping Tbs.)
Onion (2, small size)

Parsnips (2 heaping Tbs.)
Peas (2 heaping Tbs.)
Pumpkin (3 heaping Tbs.)
Rutabaga (2 heaping Tbs.)
Squash (2 heaping Tbs.)
Turnips (2 heaping Tbs.)

SALAD LIST

Tossed greens
Watercress and lettuce (romaine or bibb or head)
Radish and watercress
Celery and cabbage
Pimiento and greens
Stuffed tomato (cottage cheese, chopped celery)
Dressing should be based on pure vegetable oil: 2 or 3 tsp. per salad, once daily, with seasonings to taste

DESSERT LIST

Melon, other than watermelon (¼)
Nonfat milk and diet ginger ale, half and half
Fruit cocktail, from fruit list, small portion
Whole gelatin dessert, with genuine vanilla flavor, plus small amount fruit from list.

At luncheon *or* dinner, one level teaspoon of butter may be used on your vegetables. Lemon juice may be substituted for salad dressing when you wish to use two teaspoons of butter on vegetables. Don't make this a ritual—the vegetable oils convey nutrients you need, which butter doesn't supply.

APPETITE BRAKES

Avoid soups: they are optional anyway, and tend to stimulate appetite. Use a few protein tablets, available at health food stores, if appetite presses you between meals. Choose a brand low in carbohydrate, high in protein. Experiment until you find one which is palatable—important because most of these tablets are chewable. Generally, protein

'ates containing mixtures of several types of high-
)rotein—such as fish, eggs, egg white, nonfat milk,
yeast, lactalbumin—will be nutritionally superior
made from only one protein, and those of animal
...gin will be superior to the vegetable-cereal derived, such as soy. Protein foods act as complements to each other, for one may supply an amino acid missing from or inadequately supplied by another. That is why mixtures of protein sources in meals are better than using just one. A little protein goes a long way in checking appetite, which is the nutritionist's way of saying that it "sticks to the ribs."

Some readers who were never successful in remaining on a reducing diet have found great help from the use of bran tablets. Three or more 500 milligram tablets daily have produced a sense of satiety which has sharply bolstered will power. The number of tablets is determined not only by the lessening of hunger, but also by normalization of bowel habits. The optimal intake is that which produces evacuation without strain, and a marked deodorizing of the stool. Initially, there may be a tendency to flatulence, which will be excessive if the dose of bran is too high, but tends to lessen and disappear if the intake is proper for the individual.

REDUCING-DIET SUPPLEMENTS

Eating less food means less vitamin-mineral intake, which is one good reason for supplementing the reducing diet. A second good reason is the thesis of this book: the supplements help to control estrogen activity. A third good reason is the helpfulness of food supplements in normalizing fat distribution, as you lose weight. This is important to women who complain that however successful they are in reducing, the dimensions shrink everywhere except where they should, the face grows thin and cadaverous, but the midriff bicycle (or truck) tire remains serenely untouched. To distribute weight loss more uniformly and to retain subcutaneous fat on your face, it is sometimes helpful to supplement the reducing diet with Vitamin E, choline, inositol, and lecithin, plus the Vitamin B Complex. If your memory is well-fed, you will realize that lecithin is the only supplement in that list which you haven't encountered earlier, for the others have already been described either as antioxidants which increase resistance both to aging and to cancer, or as part of the nutritional protection against excessive estrogen activity. You will find the proper use of lecithin described later, in a summary of the instructions for supplementing both the normal menu framework and the reducing diets.

The plural *diets* is used because I must recognize the problems of a substantial group of women who don't lose weight on the usual, calorie-restricted reducing diet. They're accused of cheating because it's impossible, says the physician, to avoid weight loss on a 1,200-calorie-a-day diet unless you're hypothyroid. Not so: there are women (and men) who have a special metabolic problem which involves a unique reaction to starches and sugars. In nontechnical terms, these people have a peculiar ability to convert carbohydrates into fat, and the problem has nothing to do with the thyroid gland. They also have a tendency to store salt when they eat starches and sugars. With retention of salt comes retention of fluid. Since reducing is a process in which fat in the body is being "burned," and the oxidation of fat produces (among other by-products) water, an ordinary reducing diet which is low in calories but still relatively high in carbohydrates simply substitutes overweight from water for overweight from fat. The physician reacts to this with prescriptions for "water pills," diuretics which encourage voiding, but this is obviously treating the symptom rather than the cause. The cause is the idiosyncrasy of the patient's reaction to starches and sugars, and the remedy, obviously, is to reduce the carbohydrate content of the slimming diet from the usual 50 percent to 25 percent, more or less. This is the explanation for the popularity of the low-carbohydrate reducing diets in recent years. For those gaited for this type of nutrition, it is the only way in which they can lose weight.

These low-carbohydrate diets have encountered a storm of opposition, some of which, understandably, originated with the food establishment, which depends so largely on the sale of highly processed carbohydrate junk foods, the first to be banished in this type of reducing regimen. Less marked by such conflict of interest are the objections from well-meaning physicians and nutritionists who see a low-carbohydrate diet as automatically devolving into a high fat diet, which they equate with heart disease and hardening of the arteries. This apprehension is unjustified for two good reasons: First, the case against animal fat and cholesterol has always been founded on shaky grounds, and will be totally discredited when this medical fad has run its course. If it *were* justified, women would be as susceptible to heart attacks as men, since they eat from the same menus; yet up to menopause, women are strikingly more resistant. Second, it is not true that a low-carbohydrate diet creates a calorie vacuum into which large quantities of fat are automatically moved. Studies have shown that the satiety effect of high protein and fat intake is so great that the reducer voluntarily curbs his consumption, even when allowed unlimited amounts of the noncarbohydrate foods.

A conventional 1,200-calorie reducing diet, such as I give you in this chapter, supplies 600 calories of carbohydrates. If this portion is lowered to about 250 calories—not an earthshaking reduction—and extra protein and fat are allowed to make up the difference, the diet becomes an efficient tool for weight loss in those who have a problem with the metabolism of starch and sugar. That carbohydrate ration—250 calories, or about 60 grams—isn't a sacred figure. Some people require more—100 grams, or 400 calories—and some lose weight only by dropping the intake to 50 grams or even less. The diet which follows is therefore a starting point for those who retain fluid when they eat starch or sugar, and who find ordinary reducing diets ineffective.

In this low-carbohydrate menu framework there are several rules which *must* be observed if you want the regime to be effective. The three meals plus three snacks menus aren't optional. This diet works best with frequent small meals. The specified frequency for use of vegetable oil is also a must: despite the caloric value of such oils, they *help* you to lose weight when you're using a low-carbohydrate diet. Progress will be discouragingly slow without them. Don't try to speed up weight loss by reducing the specified portions. You may achieve your goal at the expense of feeling tired. It is necessary to stay with the recommendations for a week or two, establish your tolerance for reduced carbohydrates, and *then* experiment with the level of starch intake which strikes the best compromise between feeling well and losing weight at a satisfactory pace. Finally, the supplements used for the preceding reducing diet, plus the lecithin, are used with this diet, too. We still have our central goal: increased resistance to breast and uterine cancer. And a secondary one: normalization of the distribution of the loss of fat in the body.

It may not be necessary to remind you, but I will, that once you have reached your ideal weight, you leave the diet—whichever one you've chosen—and follow the normal menu framework, where experience will teach you how to pattern your everyday meals to keep your weight stable.

In following the low-carbohydrate diet outline, you should use reasonably:

Iodized salt
Saccharin*

*Until the controversy concerning this artificial sweetener is resolved, it is best to stop its use for an entire week, every third week, and let the material clear the system. Do not abuse saccharin, and if you are pregnant, don't use it at all.

Clear broth
Unsweetened whole gelatin
Lemon
Vinegar
All spices
Sugar-free soft drinks (not cola type) but not more than 8 oz. daily
Coffee, free of caffeine

And you should avoid:

Sugar-sweetened soft drinks, juices, and canned and frozen fruits which are sweetened
Vegetables packed in sugar-sweetened liquid or sauce (read labels carefully)
Foods with added corn sweetener, fructose, dextrose, glucose, honey, molasses
Cookies, cakes, crackers, pretzels, popcorn, potato and other types of chips, and other starch–sugar snack foods (eat nothing you wouldn't give to your baby or to your pedigreed dog).

Eat three meals and three snacks daily, with a protein food—egg, meat, fish, fowl, cheese and other protein dairy products—in each meal and snack, according to the amounts specified. Protein foods for selection are listed for you. *Don't* skip the snacks. Meal menus have been adjusted to allow for them; frequent small meals, you've learned, make weight loss easier; and the snack schedule is really built-in protection against cheating on your diet.

Each day eat one egg, cooked as you choose. If you have a good reason for avoiding eggs—allergy, or medically inflicted prohibition—substitute two ounces of meat, fish, or fowl for one egg.

Your daily intake of meat, fish, fowl and other protein foods will approximate ten to twelve ounces, cooked weight.

Don't cheat yourself: protein loses weight when cooked; a hamburger shrinks perceptibly, and so does steak. A chop weighing 5 ounces raw will weigh about 3 when cooked. Select lean meats, white fleshed fish, and poultry when you want to keep your intake of saturated fat down, though in this diet such fat does not interfere with weight loss.

If you wish, substitute ¼ cup cottage cheese for 1 ounce of meat; 1 ounce of ripened cheese (American, cheddar, Swiss, etc.) will replace 2 ounces of meat.

About 5 teaspoons of vegetable oil should be used on salad daily, and if you fall below that, take part of the oil as a supplement. It may sound distasteful, but many people do exactly that, this type of fat being so important to the weight-loss efficiency of this type of diet. The most widely available supermarket oil that is free of undesirable additives is Wesson, but in the health food store you'll find numerous pure oils which are free of these undesirable preservatives. Don't fix on one type only. Vary your selections, for oils differ widely in Vitamin E values and in their content of needed unsaturated fats. Because of the undesirable effects of hydrogenation I have ceased to recommend margarines as sources of unsaturated fats, but if you must use margarine, use the soft (not the stick) variety, which is less undesirable.

Two cups daily is the permitted amount of skim milk or partially defatted buttermilk or acidophilus milk.

You should eat two servings of fruit daily, chosen from the amounts and types specified in the following list:

Fruits	*Amount in One Serving*
Apple	1 small (2-in. diameter)
Applesauce	½ cup (no added sugar)
Apricots, fresh	2 medium
Apricots, dried	4 halves
Banana	½ small

Blackberries	1 cup
Blueberries	⅔ cup
Cantaloupe	¼ (6-in. diameter)
Cherries	10 large
Cranberries	1 cup
Dates	2
Figs, fresh	2 large
Figs, dried	1 small
Grapefruit	½ small
Grapefruit juice	½ cup
Grapes	12 large
Grape juice	¼ cup
Honeydew melon	⅛ medium
Mango	1 small
Nectarine	1 medium
Orange	1 small
Orange juice	½ cup
Papaya	⅓ medium
Peach	1 medium
Pear	1 small
Persimmon	½ small
Pineapple	½ cup
Pineapple juice	⅓ cup
Plums	2 medium
Prunes, dried	2 medium
Raspberries	1 cup
Rhubarb	1 cup
Strawberries	1 cup
Tangerine	1 cup
Watermelon	1 cup

Be warned that frozen fruits often yield more calories from sugar than from the fruit itself. Avoid canned fruits packed in syrup, whether light or heavy syrup. Choose the water-packed or artificially sweetened variety.

Eat two cups of vegetables daily, from the following list:

Asparagus
Avocado
Beet greens
Broccoli
Brussels sprouts
Cabbage
Celery
Chard
Chicory
Collards

- Cucumbers
- Dandelion
- Eggplant
- Endive
- Escarole
- Green pepper
- Green or wax beans
- Kale
- Kohlrabi
- Leeks
- Lettuce
- Mushrooms
- Mustard
- Radishes
- Sauerkraut
- Spinach
- String beans
- Summer squash
- Tomatoes
- Tomato juice
- Turnip greens
- Watercress

THE "I PROMISE TO SEE LESS OF ME" MENUS

BREAKFAST

Fruit or juice
1 egg
1 oz. meat or meat substitute, such as cheese or fish
½ slice whole-wheat bread with 1 tsp. soft margarine
1 cup weak tea, without sugar

MIDMORNING SNACK

1 cup skim milk, flavored, if desired, with vanilla or other sugar-free natural flavor
1 oz. meat or meat substitute

LUNCH

3 oz. meat (cooked weight) or meat substitute
1 serving vegetables
1 slice bread with 1 tsp. margarine
Green salad with cottonseed oil or mayonnaise (1 tsp.)
Dessert from approved selection
Weak tea or approved soft drink
NOTE: A second vegetable may be selected from the list proposed as bread substitutes.

MIDAFTERNOON SNACK

2 oz. meat or meat substitute (see snack recipes)
½ cup skim milk, flavored if desired
½ slice bread with small amount margarine

DINNER

3 oz. meat or substitute
Vegetable
Green salad, cottonseed oil or mayonnaise dressing
1 serving approved fruit
Approved dessert
Tea (weak) or other approved beverage

EVENING SNACK

½ cup skim milk, flavored if desired
1 oz. meat or meat substitute (see recipes)

SUGGESTIONS FOR BETWEEN-MEAL SNACKS

These snacks are all high in protein, though it is possible, of course, to use up some of the allotted bread intake at these little meals. To keep low the amount of carbohydrates from bread, one can use brown rice cakes, which are available in health food stores. These weigh half as much as slices of bread, and, when prewarmed, are quite palatable, satiate the craving for carbohydrates (which will lessen as the low-sugar diet is followed) at the snacks, and provide a vehicle for the protein foods.

Note that snack portions are 1 ounce—for reducers.

Cottage Cheese: a frequent choice of those on a hypoglycemia diet, can be made more palatable by adding chopped dill, chopped chives, chopped onion or scallion, shredded spinach, poppy seeds, caraway seeds, or horseradish.

Ham Horn: Press pot cheese through strainer. Add enough yogurt to make a soft paste and a little chopped dill pickle. Roll this in a paper-thin piece of ham, securing it with a toothpick to make a small horn.

Tongue–Cheese Horn: Fill paper-thin tongue slice, rolled into horn shape, with Neufchâtel cheese.

Doughless Pizza:

½ lb. lean beef
¼ small can tomato paste
2 fresh tomatoes
1 medium onion
1 pinch pepper
⅛ tsp. each of sweet basil, oregano, paprika

Pepper meat, and knead. Line small Pyrex dish with meat as substitute for pizza shell. Chop tomatoes with onions and mix with tomato paste and spices. Fill meat shell with mixture. Add a touch of oregano on top and bake to preferred doneness at 350°.

Tuna in Cucumber: Hollow out ½ cucumber, stuff with 1 oz. tuna fish mixed with 1 tsp. mayonnaise.

Cheese for Snacks: These should not be restricted in variety. Use Brie, American, cheddar, pot, farmer, cottage, and be wary only of cheese spreads, for these may be diluted with cornstarch or other carbohydrates. Gouda, Swiss, and processed cheeses (Velveeta and others of this type) are all good choices. The cheese, for variety, may be combined with another protein: ham as a blanket for a piece of Gouda is delightful, and good nutrition, too.

Celery Stick and Pot Cheese (1 oz.): Press cheese through strainer. Moisten it with a small amount of yogurt, buttermilk, or skim milk. Flavor it with chopped green pepper, watercress, parsley, or pimiento, chopped fine. Fill celery stick with mixture.

Snack Beverage: Take ½ cup plain yogurt (fruit varieties contain an unbelievable amount of sugar), and fizz it in tall glass with carbonated water (club soda) or carbonated mineral water.

Stuffed Egg Snack: Mash hard-cooked yolks of 3 eggs until fine and crumbly. Add 1 oz. melted margarine, ⅛ tsp. salt, dash pepper, ⅛ tsp. prepared mustard, ½ tsp. minced onion, 1/6 cup flaked tuna, cut-up shrimp, or crab meat. Mix until smooth, and fill hollows in egg whites, garnishing with slices of olive, pimiento, or parsley. Yields 6 stuffed-egg halves. Reducers should eat only one.

Snack Dessert and Beverage: Pour a little low-calorie ginger ale over 2 Tbs. nonfat milk powder. Use rest of soda as beverage.

Cheese–Apple Snack: Combine a wedge of Gruyère cheese with ½ small apple.

Chicken Snack: Spread 1 oz. commercial chicken spread on thin whole-wheat cracker.

Yogurt Snack: Plain yogurt (4 oz.), with vanilla or almond extract to taste.

Coleslaw Snack: 1 oz. sliced meat, such as roast beef or tongue, rolled and filled with coleslaw.

Shrimp Snack: Commercial frozen shrimp cocktail (1-oz. portion for reducers) is a convenient snack food, very rich in protein. So are canned smoked oysters.

Mushroom Snack: Stuffed mushrooms (2 oz.) filled (topped) with paste made from pot cheese, curry powder, and salt or salt substitute.

Pear Snack: Partially scoop out small pear and fill with 1 oz. soft Camembert cheese.

Hamburger: 1 oz. ground chuck with a touch of garlic, 1 tsp. tomato juice, and a dash of tarragon. Broil.

You may have up to half a slice of whole-grain bread with each meal and snack. Whole-grain crackers may be substituted, weight for weight. Don't make the mistake of omitting this bread–cracker allowance in the mistaken thought that you will necessarily speed up weight loss. You may, but you may also pay a price in fatigability and nervousness. Every person has a carbohydrate threshold, and you must use both the scale and your feeling of well-being to tell you how much—or how little—carbohydrate intake you can tolerate. The correct amount for you as a person can be quite critical. I've seen both reducers and hypoglycemics on low-carbohydrate diets for whom the addition of a small amount of starch—say, a little more bread, rice, or potato—made the difference between well-being and lack of it. As to bread substitutions, a half slice of bread may once daily be replaced by a half cup of beets, pumpkin, carrots, onions, peas, turnips, or winter squash. This is calculated in terms of carbohydrate value—not in terms of the nutrients contributed by bread, which are not provided or are less well provided by the vegetables. Such a substitution would not be possible if your intake of vitamins and minerals were not protected by the use of supplements. Bran tablets are included in the supplements to the low carbohydrate reducing diet for the same reasons which make them helpful in any reducing diet. See page 125.

Which, logically, leads us to that subject. But first, we must return to the main subject of this book, the prevention of breast cancer. It is now held that 80 percent of the incidence of cancer originates with environmental causes. Some of those carcinogenic environmental factors may interact, lending increased deadliness to the chemistries they initiate in the body. The pattern of good nutrition which builds resistance to estrogen-dependent cancer may help to protect you against other carcinogenic insults. In the next chapter, you will find the total spectrum of the use of foods, vitamins, and minerals for the best possible overall protection.

8

Protection against Invisible Menaces in the Menus

Three cancer-producing chemicals are in our diets or are synthesized by the body from precursors in our foods. One of these can be totally avoided, or if present, negated. Another can be minimized and nutritionally controlled. The third is a product of overconsumption of a popular food, a mistake easily corrected, and there are nutritional antidotes for it, too. The prerequisite for protecting yourself is knowing what you are doing when you buy, store, prepare, and consume food and when you supplement your diet. Let me provide that know-how.

Some of the food additives you've swallowed in the past twenty years are known to be capable of causing cancer. In fact, for that reason a number of them were dropped from the list of approved additives, but only after you ingested them for decades. In your food shopping, will you make a conscious effort to avoid or at least to minimize your intake of these gratuitous hazards? Before you can make that decision, you must arrive at a philosophical decision, one which, at first hand, seems unfair to inflict on a layman. Yet ultimately it is you who must decide whether to adopt the theory of *one wrong molecule,* or the opposing hypothesis, that the ability of a food chemical to cause cancer is *dose-related.* The two approaches are mutually exclusive; you hold one or the other, and your choice will make a great difference in your criteria for food shopping.

The theory of one wrong molecule holds that any single molecule of a carcinogenic chemical is a threat. Swallowing it is a risk; no dose of it is safe; there is no threshold below which it is innocuous, but above which it can cause cancer.

The theory of dose relationship says that there exists such a threshold, that what happens with high doses of chemicals will not happen at much lower levels.

If you adopt the first theory, you will be forced to make every effort to escape the minutest amounts of cancer-producing chemicals in your food and environment. If you choose the second, you will decide that you needn't worry about chloroform or other industrial chemicals in your water, or a carcinogenic dye in your cold cuts or your child's cereal, because the quantities are too small to be threatening.

There are perfectly logical, valid arguments for both of these points of view. I have had decades in which to consider them, and while I don't wish to impose my decision upon you, I do think it might be helpful to make you aware of it, and the reasoning behind it. It seems to me unlikely that one wrong molecule may cause cancer, for if that were true, I doubt that I'd be here to write these lines, or you to read them. We've all, knowingly or unknowingly, ingested *trillions* of wrong molecules; every woman has, who has taken an estrogen-based birth control pill or used lipstick containing a carcinogenic red dye. If you've eaten a licorice candy, you've swallowed a cancer-producing black coloring. If you've enjoyed a barbecued steak, you've displayed a yen for the taste which comes from the breakdown products of heated animal fats, known to be at least cocarcinogenic.

On the other hand, the dose-related thesis has its own share of problems. If you accept the doctrine that there are safe, low levels of intake of chemicals which in greater amounts are cancer-producing, you wind up—as the average American does—swallowing over 5 *pounds* of assorted food additives yearly. The amounts of these chemicals in each food are small, but the cumulative total is large. So it is with pesticide residues. It seems comforting that the legal residue of pesticides on your fruits and vegetables is a minuscule 5 parts per million, but that ceiling applies to each distinct chemical type of insect-killer used, so that you may wind up with an apple on which there are not 5 parts per million pesticide residue, but over *250* parts per million, if the grower exercises all his legal options. Not only is the total intake of these additives and pesticides disturbing, but there is also the fact that many of them have not been tested for safety at *any* dose. Even more pertinent is the way in which tests for toxicity and carcinogenicity are performed: each chemical is tested *separately*, but we ingest them *together*. Interactions are perfectly possible, even probable, and these may—we hope—reduce danger, but they also may significantly increase it.

Not only are rats not men—and don't come back with the obvious comment on that—but conditions necessary for animal experiments may make their conclusions of dubious value when applied to man. Consider a typical experiment which shows that a tablet of saccharin, suspended in a rat's bladder, causes cancer. What implications are to be found in this demonstration, other than the conclusion that it would not be wise to suspend a tablet of saccharin in your bladder? And when a scientist announces, as one recently did, that saccharin is life-shortening in rats when fed at a level of 1 percent of the animals' diet, should you totally avoid the artificial sweetener, or should you decide that this is equivalent to your drinking up to 800 bottles of saccharin-sweetened soda pop daily, which you definitely decide not to do?

I made my own decision a very long time ago. Given a choice between identical foods, one with and the other free of additives, almost by reflex I'll choose the unchemicalized product. Sometimes that choice is exercised because the use of the additive, however innocuous it seems, covers bad manufacturing techniques or faulty recipes. There are yogurts which contain nothing but milk, with, perhaps, added milk solids. There are yogurts with vegetable gum, stabilizer, or gelatin added. I prefer the manufacturer who knows the techniques for making yogurt without such additions, however harmless.

Prime in accepting the presence of additives is the purpose for which they are added. I can live without cake icing quite happily, but if I must buy an iced cake, I'll choose one which hasn't been made whiter with a coal-tar red dye, for experience has taught me that food colorings are particularly suspect. If you doubt that, obtain a list of coal-tar dyes which were approved for food use ten years ago, and trace those—a large number—found toxic or carcinogenic, with the result that, though you swallowed them for decades, they are no longer FDA-approved. I don't accept cosmetic effects as a valid reason for additives in the formula. I don't accept a synthetic preservative which is used because a natural one has been removed—which describes the substitution of BHA and BHT for Vitamin E. I'm not about to buy a "natural" cereal which is 40 percent sugar, a totally unnatural food in a totally unnatural concentration. I wouldn't bring home baby foods containing added salt or added sugar, knowing that these ingredients, which give the infant the wrong nutritional start, are incorporated solely to please the mother's perverted taste buds. Occasionally, I strike unknowns, for new additives are created faster than tests can be scheduled for them. When in doubt, I follow an axiom which my late departed friend, Adelle Davis, suggested for the average consumer: if you can't pronounce it, don't swallow it. There are, of course, additives which are not only innocent of harm, but helpful. Into this class would fall vitamins and minerals, but that doesn't mean that products enriched with a long list of these ingredients are necessarily a good buy. Supplementing the diet should not be dictated by the formulation of a cereal manufacturer, which may be something less than rational, is always incomplete, and is often overpriced.

There are two types of food chemicals for which every effort should be made to minimize intake. One of these is the nitrosamines and the other, an equally formidable and only recently recognized carcinogen, is malonaldehyde. For both of these there are nutritional antidotes with which you should be familiar.

Neither of these substances is deliberately added to foods, for the Delaney Amendment to the Food and Drug Act, which is one-wrong-molecule orientated, forbids knowing addition of carcinogens to foods. Nitrosamines are formed—both in food and when food is ingested—as a result of an interaction between protein and the additives, nitrites and nitrates, widely used in meat products. The chemical reaction produces these carcinogenic compounds, the nitrosamines, which are so potent that a single dose has been known to cause malignancies in test animals. Bacon, beef fry, ham, and frankfurters usually contain the additives, and assays have shown the presence of nitrosamines in a small percentage of such foods. In the health food stores one can find meat products without the nitrates and nitrites, though prices are high. Vitamin C is reported to interrupt the reaction, but must be present in the stomach at the time the nitrates and nitrites are consumed, since some of the conversion into nitrosamines occurs in the digestive tract. It seems paradoxical to eat a frankfurter and to follow it with 250 milligrams of Vitamin C as an antidote, and my personal preference is for nitrite- nitrate-free products.

As formidable a carcinogen, malonaldehyde is present in many of the mainstay foods in the average diet, with beef winning top "honors" for its content, higher than poultry, pork, and nonoily fish. Most dairy products other than American cheese are free of it. Fresh, frozen, and canned fruits and vegetables contain little or none. The content in meat rises with aging: freshly slaughtered beef contains less than beef which has been aged. Freezing holds the content down, with ordinary refrigeration less effective. Food wrap makes a difference: food exposed to air will develop more malonaldehyde than food in air-tight wrap. Cooking makes an unpredictable difference, usually in the direction of increasing malonaldehyde content. A sirloin tip roast which contained about 9 milligrams of the carcinogen per gram of raw meat, had 27 milligrams when roasted. Hamburger contained nearly 4 milligrams when raw and nearly 10½ when broiled. Freshly opened peanut butter did not contain the factor, but once the jar had been opened and partially used, the exposure to air created 1.2 milligrams of malonaldehyde per gram. The low content of the factor in raw chicken and turkey rose significantly when they were cooked. Apparently insignificant changes in cooking methods made for great differences in concentration of the carcinogen in the table-ready food. Thus a broiled pork chop dropped sharply in malonaldehyde content when cooked for an hour at 425° F., but when a chop was breaded and cooked at the same temperature for the same length of time, the malonaldehyde content rose sharply.

With these variables, it's unlikely that any practical technique for lowering malonaldehyde intake will be developed. Fortunately, the chemistry of its synthesis is oxygen-dependent, as you can realize from the influence of air on its development. This means that the antioxidants in nutrition should be efficient in blocking the cancer-causing activity of this ubiquitous compound, and that is the conclusion reached by the researcher who first identified this carcinogen. This is another of the reasons for the emphasis I've placed on intake of Vitamin C, Vitamin E, selenium, and other antioxidants in the diet.

That brings us to the third carcinogenic factor in American diet, the polyunsaturated fats which are used in excessive quantities. Though television and magazine advertising have persuaded you that margarine stands between your husband and a heart attack and that polyunsaturated (vegetable) oils will protect against hardening of the arteries, the fact is that *excessive* intake of such fats is at least dangerous, and possibly lethal. Not only will extensive use of such fats not provide a shield against cardiovascular diseases, but it may actually *cause* them. There is evidence, too, that excessive intake of polyunsaturates without the vital nutritional antidotes may accelerate aging and may cause cancer. It is knowledge of these effects which made it necessary for me to specify exactly how much vegetable fat should be used in your menu framework and reducing diets, and the same consideration shaped the recommendations for the use of supplements. I think it extremely important that you understand the dangers and the antidotes for them.

Let's begin by acknowledging that the vegetable oils and the margarines made from them are far from being the natural fats of the seeds from which they originated. A typical method of processing is to crush the seed under great pressure, which extracts the oil—at this stage, it is a dark substance with uninviting taste and odor. This will not please the housewife, who for esoteric reasons must be able to read the oil label from the back of the bottle, demanding a clear, transparent product which, needless to say, must taste better than the source material does. Accordingly, lye is added, to convert the free fatty acids into soap, which is discarded, and the remaining oil is now successively bleached, heated, chilled ("winterized" is the description in the advertisements) to avoid cloudiness in the oil at low temperatures, filtered through charcoal, and then put through a succession of filter presses. Any chemist will grant that there is a small chance that the finished product reflects the nutritional values of the original oil.

In another method, after the seeds are crushed, a solvent is used—anything from gasoline to ether or carbon tetrachloride—to extract the oil, and the liquid is then boiled to get rid of the solvent, some of which may remain. Then follows the lye treatment, plus superheating to deodorize the oil, with filtering as a final step. At this point, the Vitamin E natural in the oil may have been altered or removed and the processor will add a synthetic antioxidant, such as BHT or BHA, as a preservative. The presence of these additives is therefore an explicit admission that the oil doesn't contain enough of the natural preservative, Vitamin E, to protect it against rancidity.

Your problem is now simple to explain: when you store polyunsaturated fat in your cells, it is as subject to rancidity there as it is in the bottle. It is as sensitive to oxygen in the body as it is on the pantry shelf. And in the body, polyunsaturated fat exposed to oxygen breaks down into two distinct threats to well-being. These are called free radicals and dienes. A free radical is, chemically speaking, a piece torn from a molecule. It is an abnormality, and built into it is an abnormal (electrical) "drive" to unite itself with other molecules. When it does this in the cells, it upsets the sequence of chemical activities, touching off a chain of abnormal reactions which prematurely age the cell or even kill it. Moreover, one free radical begets another—many others—making it possible for just one of these molecular fragments to alter many of the chemicals of life. Don't treat this as academic, for we all, at this very minute, are aging more quickly than normal because of the attack of oxygen on these sensitive fats in our cells.

The use of polyunsaturated fats in large amounts can therefore initiate one type of hardening of the arteries—the very disorder they are popularly supposed to prevent. They can contribute to, rather than protect against, a type of heart disease—cells in the heart can die prematurely, too. And they can cause the body to change normal life chemicals into alien compounds, which not only fail to participate in the chemistry of life, but act as carcinogens.

Dienes are a second threat deriving from overuse of polyunsaturates in the absence of sufficient antioxidant protection. They are specific fragments of polyunsaturates which can help to form free radicals, or of themselves damage the cells. Since adequate blood levels of Vitamin E will restrain the formation of dienes, blood tests for these factors are a way of detecting a deficiency in the vitamin, and it is revealing that tests for dienes in our polyunsaturated-saturated public have often shown Vitamin E deficiency. Those of you who know that oils usually contain Vitamin E will be puzzled: why doesn't the natural content of the vitamin stop the formation of free radicals and dienes? The answer: the fat is stored in the cells. It isn't transient in the body, as some other types of fat may be, and the oxygen attack on it isn't transient either, but continuous, in the course of which the Vitamin E in the oil is literally used up. The role of the vitamin as an expendable protection is analogous to the heat shield on a returning space ship, which is sacrificed to protect the ship from burning up in the atmosphere. So it is that fresh supplies of the vitamin must be continuously available, if the fat is to be protected against the active oxygen which can cause formation of dienes and free radicals; and the need for the vitamin rises as the intake of the oil does. The amount of Vitamin E natural to the oil may not be sufficient for such protection against oxidation, and the intense processing to which the oil is subjected may seriously deplete the Vitamin E content. It also depletes the lecithin content—lecithin being one of the natural antioxidants which, unfortunately, darken the natural oil, making it unattractive to the housewife.

The processes by which margarine is made from these

fats carry the alteration of the natural food still further. On margarine labels, you will see the term "partially hydrogenated," and you should understand what that means. A vegetable fat has the capacity to accept additional hydrogen in its molecular structure. The more hydrogen it is willing to accept, the more "unsaturated" (with hydrogen) it was in the first place. Conversely, a saturated fat is one which has combined to the maximum with hydrogen. In partial hydrogenation, the vegetable fat is brought only partially toward the saturated stage by incorporation of hydrogen in the molecule. Full hydrogenation would turn the oil into a solid fat; the partial process creates a semisolid, suited to be used as a spread for bread. If we must consider that the original vegetable fat has been subjected to drastic changes in processing, the techniques in margarine manufacture carry the alienation an additional step. In partial hydrogenation, quantities of a "halfway" type of fat are created, which may present metabolic problems for the body.

The soft margarines are preferable to the solid type, though either will, like the vegetable oils, create a continuing need for Vitamin E and other antioxidants. I have a lingering suspicion, which I've not yet been able to confirm, that some of these margarines are made from vegetable oil residues from the manufacture of Vitamin E concentrates. If so, they are obviously devoid of the vitamin, while increasing the need.

In general, it will be better to choose the "cold-pressed" oils which you will find in the health food stores as sources of unsaturated fat, rather than the margarines. Don't overlook your need for this type of fat. It is important to cell membranes, vital in body chemistry, a necessary starting point for the body's manufacture of quasi-hormone factors known as prostaglandins. Such fats may be needed to prevent disorders which, like multiple sclerosis, strip the insulation from the nerves. Such fats contain factors important to nerve cells in the brain, too.

Previous discussion of the antioxidants acquainted you with Vitamin E, selenium, Vitamin C, and the sulfur-containing proteins. To keep the dienes and free radicals muzzled, the first step is to avoid excessive use of unsaturated fats, and the second is to assure your intake of that list of antioxidants, to which a few more should now be added. The list should also include Vitamin A, biotin, lecithin, and Vitamin B_{12}. It's interesting that eggs, so long maligned by anticholesterol faddists, are good sources of every one of these protective factors, save Vitamin C.

SOURCES OF ANTIOXIDANTS AND OTHER PROTECTIVE FACTORS

Selenium

As critical to cancer resistance as this nutrient is, it is ironic that supplements of selenium were added to animal feeds decades before they were made available to the public. Soil levels of selenium vary so much that it's impossible to depend on just a few foods for this essential nutrient, for the grazing animal, like the vegetable, can't be a rich source of a factor in which the soil is very poor. Good sources of selenium include brewer's yeast, garlic, liver, eggs, onions, asparagus, tuna, mushrooms, shrimp, kidney, and whole grains. Highly refined foods lose large percentages of their selenium, a good example being white rice, which has one fifteenth the selenium value of brown rice, and white bread, which has half the value of whole-wheat. Selenium alone, incorporated in yeast, or combined with Vitamin E, with which it helpfully interacts, is now available in supplements in the health food stores. Label instructions for dosage should be followed, for excessive intake of selenium (like excessive intake of anything else) can be toxic. The usual range of supplementary intake is from 50 to 150 micrograms ($^1/_6$ milligram) daily. It's a minute amount, but don't underestimate its potency in raising resistance to cancer.

Vitamin E

I am frequently asked whether one should use wheat-germ oil *or* Vitamin E. The question reflects a popular misunderstanding, for wheat-germ oil contains Vitamin E, but also contains many factors besides the vitamin. It isn't synonymous with Vitamin E. Beneficial effects from wheat-germ oil may derive from factors other than Vitamin E, and it doesn't contain enough of the vitamin to serve as a useful supplement of it. One uses wheat-germ oil *and* Vitamin E supplements. Wheat germ oil may be added to your salad oil. Its flavor is too strong for some palates, but diluted in this way it is acceptable. Use one part wheat germ oil and three parts salad oil for salads—not for cooking.

Vitamin E appears in four forms which are useful to us in different ways. One of those ways is *not* aphrodisiac action—Vitamin E is not the middle letter in the word *sex*. Alpha tocopherol is the form of Vitamin E that has an important role in the internal energy chemistry of the cells. It is the anticlotting agent that helps users of the Pill to avoid clots and the strokes and thrombophlebitis that are caused by them. The other three forms of the vitamin—the beta, gamma, and delta tocopherols—have their most pronounced effect as antioxidants, and you now know how important that effect is in protecting us against the untoward actions of the dienes and free radicals. All forms of the vitamin—alpha, beta, gamma, and delta—are important if you want a healthy heart. You therefore do not buy alpha tocopherol alone to use as a supplement. You buy mixed tocopherols. The activity of the supplement will be stated in thus-and-so-many units or milligrams of alpha tocopherol; the content in beta, gamma, and delta will not be listed, but their presence is guaranteed by the phrase "mixed tocopherols" on the label.

In addition to the importance of Vitamin E as an antioxidant, it has other roles which serve the special needs of women, for it is an antidote for some of the side reactions to the Pill, and for many women, it cushions the troublesome years of the menopause, often reducing anxiety, nervousness, and the vasomotor disturbances (sweats and flushes) of the menopause—without the carcinogenic effects of the estrogens.

Before I suggest appropriate levels of intake, let me note that hypertensives should take Vitamin E under medical supervision. There is an idiosyncrasy of reaction in a small percentage of those with high blood pressure, in which the vitamin may cause a small rise in the pressure. For them, the initial dose is held below 100 international units of Vitamin E daily, and raised each month to the desired level, with checks of the pressure before each increment in dosage. Heart disease should not be self-treated with the vitamin. Though thousands of laymen have done this for themselves, for angina, and with great benefit, there are risks for those with heart failure or rheumatic heart disease. In heart failure, which is usually on the left side of the heart, the right, less troubled side may be the first to respond to the vitamin, thereby increasing the difference in the efficiency of the two sides, with consequent difficulties. In rheumatic heart disease, the condition of the heart valve will determine the dosage, and that obviously must be monitored by a physician competent in such therapy. In diabetes, the vitamin often reduces insulin requirement, which is fine, but the readjustment again requires medical supervision. As against these negative points, you should know that studies of those using between 400 and 800 units of Vitamin E daily, for long periods, show approximately 99 percent less heart disease than would be found in a similar group of Americans not using the vitamin.

For those who are healthy and would like to stay that way—and who are not using any medication with which the vitamin might interact, such as insulin, anticoagulants, or digitalis or other heart drugs—400 to 1,200 units of Vitamin E daily, in the form of mixed tocopherols, would make nutritional sense. The best procedure is to start lower, with 100 units daily, and gradually increase, until you find the supplementary intake which helps you to feel most fit. You will find it comforting to realize that this simple step erects a nutritional shield against the chemistry of cancer from free radicals, dienes, and malonaldehyde. Those who use it prior to and during the menopause, thereby preventing or mitigating the disturbances of those years in a woman's life, also have the comfort of knowing that the vitamin, unlike the estrogens, is harmless. And the effectiveness of Vitamin E in helping to retard aging is very real. I know it to be partially responsible for the startling prolongation of the prime of life of some of the famous people you envy because they seem to be ageless.

Though plastic surgeons have been slow to adopt the technique, it will be of interest for you to know that application of Vitamin E—squeezed out of the capsules—to burns and injuries has reduced pain markedly and mitigated scarring, and in some spectacular cases has avoided the need for plastic surgery after severe burns. The vitamin also has therapeutic uses in arthritis, bursitis, and other painful and disabling disorders, for which medical nutritionists utilize it as part of their treatments. Since good nutrition often mitigates or prevents what it helps or cures, the moral is that those who raise their intake of Vitamin E may enjoy the dividends most difficult to identify: what doesn't happen.

Sulfur

You will recall that the sulfur-containing amino acids were listed among the important antioxidants. Amino acids are the building blocks of protein; everything from lamb chops to fish to cheese to your own tissues represents a collection of amino acids.

Your sulfur supply ordinarily comes from protein foods which contain the types of amino acids which in turn contain sulfur. There are four of these, one which is obtainable only from the diet and three which are made from that one, in the body. The fourth—the one sulfur-containing amino acid which the body can't make for itself—is methionine, supplements of which are used to aid liver function. In fact, when we wish to accelerate the process of liver degradation of estrogen, we may give supplements of methionine to speed the response. I have already pointed out that eggs are among the very few foods rich in sulfur-containing amino acids, which means that those who fall prey to the misguided low cholesterol diet, which usually forbids eggs, may become deficient in sulfur. Beef proteins (meaning steaks, chops, and other muscle meats) supply a little sulfur; onion and garlic supply more. It would appear that for some people, grandmother's sulfur and molasses might make sense, but we have no such supplements on the market, though for a person who doesn't eat eggs, they might be protective. It is possible for the physician to prescribe sulfur supplements for those who can't or won't eat eggs, by having the druggist follow the suggestion of Dr. Carl Pfeiffer of the Brain Bio Center to fill No. 1 capsules with flowers of sulfur. One capsule, once daily, will provide about 200 milligrams of sulfur, which is about 25 percent of the requirement, the rest obtainable from the normal content in the diet of the sulfur-containing amino acids—except for vegetarians and others who don't eat eggs and meat.

Small doses of sulfur are sometimes helpful in psoriasis and, either in supplementary form or fed in eggs, sulfur has been recommended in rheumatoid arthritis. Egg yolks or supplements of sulfur are also used to help normalize the bacterial flora of the bowel after antibiotic therapy. Sulfur is frequently added to animal feed, for cattle, chickens, and pigs, so that we see with this nutrient what we did with selenium: the human need neglected, the animal need carefully guarded. Our prime interest in sulfur is the role of antioxidant played by the amino acids which supply this nutritional factor.

Repeated references to eggs as a good source of all antioxidants, save Vitamin C, and repeated criticisms of the low-cholesterol diet which forbids or precariously limits the intake of this superb food, demand a parting look at the latest insult from the processed-food industry: egg substitutes. A typical product, labeled as a cholesterol-free egg substitute, is made from corn oil, egg white, nonfat dry milk, emulsifiers, gums, preservatives, artificial flavor, aluminum sulfate, artificial color, iron phosphate, and three added vitamins, thiamin, riboflavin, and Vitamin D. This triumph of technology over nature no longer supplies usable sulfur, has lost virtually all of its zinc, no longer contains Vitamin B_6, is no longer a source of Vitamin A (an important anticancer factor), and is bankrupt in the trace minerals and other nutrients (which the baby chick needs as we do). The amputated egg yolks wind up in—you guessed it—pet foods, cosmetics, and some bakery products. A short description of this "egg substitute": it has lost the antioxidants which help to protect you against cancer. It is a striking example of the blindness of food technology to the nutritional needs of the public it exploits.

Lecithin

Known in nutrition as a phosphatide, this natural factor in oils (which is also manufactured in the body) is an antioxidant which is removed from polyunsaturated fats. In the body, lecithin has a variety of critical functions, one of which involves fat transport and control of cholesterol. Ordinarily, the body's synthesis of lecithin is adequate to meet its needs, but certain precursors must be supplied in requisite amounts, these including Vitamin B_6, magnesium, choline, and polyunsaturated fats. You ordinarily obtain adequate lecithin from foods like eggs, milk, and soybeans, but many consumers take supplements of the factor, primarily as an aid in avoiding or minimizing deposition of cholesterol on the walls of the arteries. I have the impression that supplements of lecithin have sometimes been useful in augmenting the efficiency of the liver in controlling estrogen activity. It is also useful in improving the utilization of fat-soluble vitamins, A, D, E, and K, and has been helpful to individuals with poor tolerance for fats in the diet. It is available in granules, which some people take in cereal or tomato juice; and it is also marketed in 1,200-milligram capsules. Six of the capsules or a tablespoonful of the granules are roughly equivalent, and constitute a supplementary intake of the factor.

Vitamin A

Though our older citizens remember taking cod-liver oil as children—and high-grade cod liver oil contains as much as 30,000 units of Vitamin A per teaspoonful—the FDA, on totally irrelevant considerations, decided to limit the potency of Vitamin A capsules to 10,000 units. Since nothing prevents you from taking 2 or 200 of these capsules at once, it is a little difficult to understand why this limitation is supposed to protect us against toxicity. Actually, the *need* of some people for Vitamin A exceeds 25,000 units daily. This isn't academic, for adequate intake of the vitamin has been found to be protective against cancer. To add to the problem of supplements limited in Vitamin A potency, the public—via the low-cholesterol diet—has been encouraged to abstain from foods rich in the vitamin, such as liver, cream, eggs, and butter. The high value of Vitamin A in foods like parsley, spinach, and watercress is an illusion. These foods do not contain the vitamin, but supply a precursor which the body converts into the vitamin. Some people are inefficient in that conversion, while diabetics fail in it almost completely. Your multiple vitamin supplement, which is part of your system of estrogen controls, will usually supply 10,000 units of Vitamin A. But I think you should know that there are people who refuse to fit into the biochemical straitjacket of the tables of "recommended dietary allowances" published by government agencies, and who may need more Vitamin A in their supplements than do other people. The range of requirements for the vitamin actually goes from about 5,000 units daily to about 33,000, according to the best studies available.

Biotin

Biotin, like choline and inositol, is a lipotropic factor—a substance involved in fat metabolism—and, as such, is of interest to us when we are concerned with liver regulation of estrogen. There is an interrelationship between inositol and biotin: the synthesis of biotin by intestinal bacteria seems to be dependent, in part, on the presence of inositol. The synthesized supply may be larger than the amount received from the diet, originating in egg yolk, organ meats, yeast, legumes (peas, beans), and nuts, with small amounts in muscle meats and milk. We need about 150 micrograms daily—about one sixth of a milligram—and a well-balanced diet should supply somewhere between this figure and 300 micrograms daily. Biotin is incorporated in some multiple vitamin supplements and, more frequently, in Vitamin B Complex concentrates.

Vitamin B_{12}

Unless one is on a purely vegetarian diet, intake of Vitamin B_{12} is likely to be adequate, since it is supplied by such protein foods as meat, poultry, eggs, fish, cheese, and brewer's yeast, with very rich supplies in such seafoods as shrimp, oysters, and clams. Our interest in Vitamin B_{12} stems from its action in the body in synthesis of other factors which are lipotropes, and thereby affect liver function. Most multiple and Vitamin B Complex supplements supply useful amounts of this vitamin, deficiency in which is more likely to originate with poor utilization than in inadequate dietary supplies (except, as I noted, in vegetarianism).

Vitamin C

Unlike other antioxidants, Vitamin C has (recently) demonstrated remarkable helpfulness in the *treatment* of cancer, prolonging the survival of terminal patients by a considerable factor, and in a number of cases, appearing to have brought the disease into complete remission. But we—you and I—are interested in prevention, and the therapeutic effect of this vitamin in terminal cancer does open the door to even more useful effects if it is given in earlier cancer, and still more useful action if taken as an antioxidant which is unusual in that it also stimulates the white blood cells, which must battle intruders ranging from bacteria to cancer cells. (You will find a full discussion of this effect of ascorbic acid in Chapter 5.)

While the terminal cancer cases were given 10,000 milligrams (10 grams) of Vitamin C daily—and intake this high for healthy people who want to stay that way has been recommended by some nutritionists—Dr. Linus Pauling, who must know more about this vitamin than any of us, suggests that the range of everyday requirement extends from 250 milligrams daily to 2,500. If a cold threatens to break through, he recommends larger amounts—5 or 10 grams daily. These doses sound astronomical, but they are small in comparison with the doses used in treating hepatitis, serious viral infections, and schizophrenia.

There is no way to obtain this intake of Vitamin C from food: one would drown in citrus juice, and most multiple supplements don't supply 250 milligrams and upward. This means that adjunct supplementing with the individual vitamin is necessary, exactly as it is with Vitamin E.

Vitamin B_6

Because estrogen—whether supplied by the Pill or the ovaries or a prescription drug—elevates the need for Vitamin B_6, and because this vitamin can sharply reduce the water retention and other premenstrual and menstrual disturbances, I must call your attention to the differences in the content of Vitamin B_6 in Vitamin B Complex supplements. In addition to being sure that they supply enough choline and inositol, which many products don't, you should make sure that they supply at least 10 milligrams of Vitamin B_6 (pyridoxin) in the recommended daily dose. If not, the vitamin, like Vitamin C and Vitamin E, can be taken separately.

Inositol

You know why this factor—not recognized as a vitamin—is a very important member of the Vitamin B Complex for a woman. Its action in helping liver control of estrogen isn't its only beneficial effect. Just as an example of another dividend: Patients treated with inositol are often able to drop the use of tranquilizers, according to the Brain Bio Center, for the effect of the factor on the brain waves is curiously close to that of the drugs, without making the person sleepy or vegetative. Be sure your Vitamin B Complex supplement supplies 500 milligrams of inositol. It doesn't matter if there is a little more, but there shouldn't be less. There are such supplements available, but should you have difficulty in locating one, additional inositol can be taken separately. If you are taking lecithin, this will supply some inositol, and the 500-milligram figure can be reduced to about 300.

Choline

Again, you have learned of the importance of choline in helping liver control of estrogen. It has other beneficial effects, including helping in the utilization of fats, and it is important that your Vitamin B Complex supplement provide 1,000 milligrams (1 gram) of choline in the recommended daily intake. If you are using lecithin, you will have an adjunct source of both choline and inositol from it, and can reduce the amount of choline in the B Complex supplement by about one third—to about 650 milligrams daily.

The Vitamin B Complex Supplement

Just by way of example, the following is a typical B Complex formula, available in health food stores. You will note that it supplies more inositol than is needed (which isn't a fault); that it contains less Vitamin B_6 than I have specified (which should be augmented with a separate tablet); and that its content of folic acid and PABA are within the limits I have specified.

Vitamin B Complex, high choline and inositol in a natural base (natural coated/sugarless)

An especially designed formula, providing well-balanced amounts of the B Complex vitamins together with high-potency levels of the associated lipotropic (fat-mobilizing) B factors, choline and inositol, all prepared in natural-coated, sugarless tablets and combined synergistically in a natural base containing brewer's yeast, lecithin, nucleic acid, rice bran, wheat germ, and whey, contributing additional trace nutrients.

Each six tablets provide:

Choline bitartrate	1,000 mg.
Inositol (from corn)	1,000 mg.
Vitamin B_1 (thiamine mononitrate)	5 mg.
Vitamin B_2 (riboflavin)	5 mg.
Vitamin B_6 (pyridoxine HCl)	5 mg.
Niacinamide	50 mg.
Vitamin B_{12} (cobalamin conc. NF)	25 mcg.
Folic acid	100 mcg.
d-Biotin	30 mcg.
Pantothenic acid (as calcium pantothenate)	100 mg.
Para-aminobenzoic acid	30 mg.

Multiple Vitamin–Mineral Supplement

There follows a typical formula, available in health food stores. You will note that the Vitamin E is far below the level recommended, which calls for additional intake of the vitamin in a separate capsule. The B_6 content is excellent, making up for the deficit in the Vitamin B Complex formula. The Vitamin C is at the minimum level specified, and may require augmenting with a separate supplement of ascorbic acid, if you find that higher intake of this vitamin brings dividends for you. The PABA and folic acid values augment those of the B Complex formula, bringing them a little higher than I had wanted, but it is difficult to avoid that, and the difference isn't precarious if the inositol and choline intakes are adequate. This formula supplies iodine, making it unnecessary to use iodized salt or kelp tablets. The Vitamin A value is midway, above the minimum requirement, but below the optimal for some people, who would have to use a separate supplement. (If you keep our objectives in mind, you won't find all this too demanding.)

High-potency, one-per-day multiple vitamins and chelated minerals in a natural base (natural coated/ sugarless)

A high-potency vitamin and mineral formula, derived from natural and organic sources and prepared in natural-coated, sugarless tablets. One tablet per day supplies ample potencies of all the essential vitamins plus the essential minerals in chelated form, synergistically combined with a natural base of acerola, alfalfa, bone meal, ginseng, kelp, lecithin, nucleic acid, papaya, and rice bran, with desiccated stomach substance to facilitate Vitamin B_{12} absorption.

Each tablet provides:

Vitamin A (from fish liver oil)	10,000 USP units
Vitamin D (from fish liver oil)	400 USP units

Vitamin E	
(d-Alpha tocopheryl acid succinate)	24.8 mg./30IU
Vitamin C (with rose hips)	250 mg.
Citrus bioflavonoid complex	25 mg.
Rutin (from eucalyptus)	25 mg.
Hesperidin complex	5 mg.
Vitamin B_1 (thiamine mononitrate)	25 mg.
Vitamin B_2 (riboflavin)	25 mg.
Vitamin B_6 (pyridoxine HCl)	25 mg.
Niacinamide	100 mg.
Vitamin B_{12} (cobalamin conc. NF)	100 mcg.
Folic acid	100 mcg.
d-Biotin	20 mcg.
Choline bitartrate	150 mg.
Inositol (from corn)	150 mg.
Pantothenic acid (as calcium pantothenate)	100 mg.
Para-aminobenzoic acid	25 mg.
Iron peptonate	50 mg.
Calcium (from bone meal)	40 mg.
Magnesium chelate (gluconate)	7 mg.
Manganese chelate (gluconate)	6 mg.
Copper chelate (gluconate)	0.25 mg.
Zinc (as gluconate chelate)	0.18 mg.
Potassium iodide	0.1 mg.
Desiccated liver	50 mg.
Betaine HCl	25 mg.
L-Lysine HCl (from fermentation ext.)	10 mg.

Another Type of Multiple Vitamin–Mineral Supplement

Some manufacturers, aware that the birth control pill has created an increased need for certain vitamins, have created supplements to meet those needs, of which the following formula is an example. Unfortunately, manufacturers do *not* know that inositol and choline are important in estrogen control, too. The omission of these factors would, of course, demand their use separately.

Specially formulated Multi-vitamin/mineral for the modern woman (High Vitamin B_6, Vitamin C, Vitamin E, and zinc)

A special formulation of essential vitamins and minerals designed to provide for the increased nutritional needs of the modern woman, supplying the important Vitamin B_6 at high potency and ample quantities of Vitamin C, Vitamin E, and zinc—all derived from natural materials, including dolomite, fish liver oils, rose hips, and selected high-potency yeasts.

Each two tablets provide:

Vitamin A (from fish liver oil)	5,000 USP units
Vitamin D (from fish liver oil)	400 USP units
Vitamin E (d-Alpha tocopheryl acid succinate)	24.8 mg./30 IU
Vitamin C (with rose hips)	200 mg.
Vitamin B_1 (from yeast conc.)	1.5 mg.
Vitamin B_2 (from yeast conc.)	1.8 mg.
Vitamin B_6 (pyridoxine HCl)	50 mg.
Niacin (from yeast conc.)	20 mg.
Vitamin B_{12} (cobalamin conc. NF)	25 mcg.
Folic acid	100 mcg.
Pantothenic acid (as calcium pantothenate)	50 mg.
Calcium (from dolomite)	100 mg.
Magnesium (from dolomite)	60 mg.
Iron (as peptonate)	18 mg.
Zinc (as gluconate chelate)	15 mg.

The following formula is an example of a supplement to the formula above, providing a separate source of choline and inositol. You will note the presence of methionine in this formula. It is included for reasons I have touched on earlier—the helpful effect of methionine on liver function, augmenting that of inositol and choline.

High-Potency Lipotropics

A unique formulation designed to supply high-potency levels of the lipotropic (fat-mobilizing) factors—choline, inositol, and methionine.

Each three tablets contain:

Choline bitartrate	1,000 mg.
Inositol (from corn)	1,000 mg.
Methionine	300 mg.

Let me make it plain that I am concerned only with formulations, not with brand names. Regulation of the industry is rigorous, and all brands of vitamins will live up to their label potencies, but formulae count very much, as you must now know. Read labels carefully, and pick the least costly brand that meets the specifications. There is nothing wrong with mail-order vitamins, properly formulated; nothing wrong with health food store vitamins, properly formulated. I do have a preference for brands made without preservatives, coal-tar dyes, and sugar, and you will find a number which exclude these undesirable ingredients.

Don't consider supplements as license for poor nutrition. They are supplements, not substitutes.

Brewer's Yeast and Desiccated Liver

These superior foods were reviewed, with wheat germ and bran, in Chapter 7, but I want to remind you, now that you understand the importance of the antioxidants, that they supply selenium as well as methionine, plus a chromium factor which helps the metabolism of carbohydrate, an important contribution because deviations from the normal in the body's management of starches and sugars are linked with cancer. When you consider that both are also excellent sources of natural Vitamin B Complex—including the unknown factors—plus high-quality protein, you can see how much they contribute to the nutritional defenses against estrogen-dependent (and other types of) cancer.

Yogurt Versus Other Types of Fermented Milks

The bacterial flora of the lower intestine have theoretically been linked to the incidence of breast cancer. It is proposed that this type of cancer may in part be dependent on the composition of the intestinal bacterial population. Under certain circumstances—too complex for prolonged discussion—the nature of this bacterial colony can be changed so that they produce estrogen, which is absorbed, and adds to the body burden of the hormone. Though yogurt is the average nutritionist's first thought when changing bacterial flora is the goal, the fact—recently recognized—is that the type of friendly bacteria in yogurt is difficult to implant in the human intestine. More successful is the use of acidophilus milks other than the Bulgarian type which yogurt represents. This would suggest the use of such products as kefir or the new "sweet" type of acidophilus milk, which lacks the tartness usually associated with such products. There is no way to appraise the validity of this hypothesis at this moment, but the normal menu framework calls for milk and milk products, kefir, and equivalent products, and acidophilus milk can be substituted for the everyday variety. Any hope of success in changing bacterial flora will be predicated on everyday use of such sources of friendly bacteria. Incidentally, when your quick lunch includes that long-time penance of the overweight, cottage cheese, you can convert it into a delightful treat by stirring in one of the kefirs flavored with natural fruit, sans added sugar. Brands are available in some areas.

RAISING YOUR NUTRITIONAL UMBRELLA

Before you launch your application of nutrition versus breast and uterine cancer, there is an important preliminary step: make sure you're in normal health, and that calls for a thorough medical checkup.

Your next step is to choose the food plan you will follow, the normal framework or, if needed, one of the reducing diets, with which you stay until you reach your ideal weight, defined as that at which you feel and function best. You then revert to the normal framework, a lifetime program which, with such adjustments as your scale dictates, should keep you at that ideal weight.

You implement this by sitting down and making a careful list of the changes needed in your criteria for food shopping. Where you bought ordinary breakfast cereals before, you will be buying whole-grain cereals now, with a careful eye on the label for undesirable additives. Your white bread, unless you need it for cleaning suede shoes, parchment lampshades, and typewriter keys, will give way to whole-wheat bread. You'll be buying bran (or, if it is your preference, bran tablets). You have a new list at the meat counter. Unless medically and flatly prohibited, you'll be buying more eggs. In short, you'll be following all the suggestions you've picked up in this book, with necessary modifications for personal idiosyncrasies of tolerances and needs. For foods, you will first prepare your revised shopping list for the supermarket. Your health food store list will follow, comprising the foods and supplements these shops uniquely supply. If there are no such stores in your area, find your way to one which will serve you by mail, which many will.

In the health food store, you'll find the multiple vitamin, single vitamin, multiple mineral, and Vitamin B Complex supplements you need. When the multiple or the B Complex fall short of needed levels of critical factors, you will choose individual supplements to make up the differences. At the same time you'll buy your supplies of brewer's yeast and desiccated liver, remembering that these are foods and there is no actual "dose." If you must have a guideline more precise than "a handful of tablets," use fifteen of each daily—five after a meal, three times daily. You'll also buy wheat germ, undefatted, and if available, vacuum-packed.

Rotate your choices of vegetable oils, buying them in small bottles and keeping them in the refrigerator. Although I count good nutrition as cheaper than crisis medicine, be sure to keep an eye on prices: the less costly of two identical formulae should be chosen, of course, but only so long as you are not penalized with undesirable preservatives and dyes. The brands which omit such ingredients usually announce the fact on their labels.

Give your body at least four months of this good food and these helpful supplements. You'll want to continue if you respond as about seven in ten women do, with tangible evidence that the betterment of your diet is helping the body to readjust the ratio between estrogen and estriol, for as excessive estrogen levels fall, menstruation may—and often does—appear without warning, the premenstrual week loses its terrors, heavy hemorrhaging is reduced, and the duration of the flow may be three days instead of five.

Further evidence that you are taming a killer hormone may be provided by an improvement in cystic mastitis—a triumph of nutritional chemistry which your doctor will certainly want to—and should be—given the opportunity to monitor, for this is the only way in which he will be motivated to pass this information on to other women.

There may be other dividends, too, in the appearance of nails, hair, and skin; in improved muscle tone, in circulation, in elimination; in rising resistance to infection and to fatigue. But as significant and important as these responses may be (and should be) to the average woman, to me they are routine reactions to improved nutrition. The prime goal still beckons imperiously: what doesn't happen.

9

Supplements: The Dietary Insurance Policy

Far more efficient than vegetable oils in lowering blood cholesterol is old-fashioned cod-liver oil, but the baby of today receives only the Vitamins A and D of that oil. I cite this not only because this deprivation may be harmful to infants, but because it emphasizes the fact that there is no such thing as a perfect vitamin supplement. The fault may lie in what we leave behind when we concentrate a natural factor. It may be that the synthesized vitamin lacks the helpful fellow-traveling trace substances which in nature accompany the natural vitamin. It may be—and assuredly is—that there are unknown factors in food which our supplements obviously won't contain. It is for that reason that I caution you not to use vitamin concentrates as a license for poor nutrition. In other words, don't let this nutritionist hear you say, however apologetically, "Well, it doesn't matter if I sin—I'm taking supplements." We try to write as complete a vitamin-mineral insurance policy for the diet as we can, but we must recognize the limitations of these concentrates. They are *supplements*, which means what it says; they aren't substitutes for good nutrition, but protective adjuncts to it.

Within these limitations, the supplements give you valuable and indispensable services. They cover deficits of vitamins and minerals discarded or destroyed in food processing. They offset vitamins inactivated by prolonged storage or exposure to light and air. They compensate for the deficits created in foods by poor soils and by fertilization aimed at quantity rather than quality of the crops. They offer insurance against some of our errors in food selection, when the pleasures of the palate take precedence over the needs of the organism. They provide assurance in the face of the unknowns you encounter when you dine away from home. To a useful extent, they may compensate for poor absorption or impaired utilization of nutrients. And, most important and most pertinent to the goal of this book, they allow a woman to raise her efficiency in control of estrogen without eating excessive amounts of food.

The preceding sentence spells out the problems created by a modern woman's running battle with calories. There is a calorie ceiling which she doesn't want to bump against, for the penalty is weight gain. But there is also a calorie floor, imposed because no matter how intelligently food is selected, intake of critical nutrients will be inadequate if you drop below that lower calorie limit. The example with iron, given earlier, perfectly illustrates this point: to achieve her iron requirement, a woman must eat more food than she is willing to consume, being more concerned with excess weight than she is with deficiency in hemoglobin. The situation with choline, inositol, and Vitamin B_6 is identical—even when her goal is control of a cancer-producing hormone, many a woman isn't willing to follow menus which may take her from a size 6 to a size 12. The vitamin-mineral supplements are perfectly adequate answers to the problem, for they raise the intake of the critical nutrients without imposing a calorie tax.

The following is representative of another modern multiple vitamin-mineral supplement, which is part of the basic procedure in assuring adequate intake of the factors critical in maintaining control of estrogen activity by the liver. A concentrate as complete as this will, of course, make up for other deficits in the dietary supply of the nutrients.

MULTIPLE VITAMIN–MINERAL SUPPLEMENT

Vitamin A: 7,500 to 10,000 units
Vitamin D: 400 units
Vitamin E: 40 units
Vitamin C: 250 mgs
B_1 (thiamin): 2 mgs
B_2 (riboflavin): 2 mgs
B_6 (pyridoxin): 3 mgs
B_{12}: (cyanocobalamin) 10 mcgs
B_3 (niacinamide): 20 mgs
Pantothenic acid (D-calcium pantothenate): 15 mgs
Biotin: .3 mgs
Folic acid: 200 mcgs
Choline (bitartrate): 250 mgs
Inositol: 250 mgs
PABA (para-aminobenzoic acid): 30 mgs
Rutin (or bioflavonoids): 200 mgs
Calcium (phosphate): 250 mgs
Phosphorus (calcium phosphate): 250 mgs
Magnesium (carbonate): 200 mgs
Iron (ferrous fumarate): 15 mgs
Zinc (gluconate): 15 mgs
Copper (sulfate): 1 mg
Iodine (kelp): .15 mgs
Manganese (gluconate): 5 mgs
Chromium (chromic sulfate): 1 mg
Selenium (dioxide): .02 mgs

In representative brands, such a formula is available in pills, sometimes chewable, and in capsules, without artificial preservatives or dyes. To achieve the potencies listed, the dose often necessary is six tablets daily for adults and teenagers. On this scale, two will be recommended for children under six, and four for children between six and twelve. Dedicated as I am (and this book is) to prevention, I should much prefer to begin nutritional prophylaxis for girls long before they reach puberty.

If we examine this supplement in terms of our goals for control of estrogen activity, we find deficits in Vitamin B_6 (pyridoxin), inositol, and choline. In terms of antioxidants, it is adequate in selenium, has the bare minimum of Vitamin C, and falls short both in quantity and varieties of Vitamin E.

We overcome these deficits by adding other supplements. The inositol and choline potencies can be brought up by use of an additional B Complex concentrate supplying enough of these factors to bring the inositol intake, from both supplements, to at least 500 milligrams daily, and the choline to 1,000 milligrams. (In nutrition, we are concerned with falling short, but not with small overages.) If the combination of the multiple and Vitamin B Complex supplements does not supply 25 milligrams of Vitamin B_6—important for the woman who is on the Pill or whose menstruation brings water retention—we can add an additional tablet of Vitamin B_6 to make up the deficit.

An alternate method of compensating for the inositol-choline shortage in the multiple supplement is the use of a separate lipotropic concentrate. A typical one might supply from 500 to 1,000 milligrams of choline and of inositol, plus a small amount of methionine. To supply these potencies the recommended dose may be three tablets daily, but because you already have inositol and choline in the multiple concentrate, you will use appropriately less of the lipotropic formula.

Up to this point, you are taking a multiple vitamin-mineral supplement. You have added a Vitamin B Complex concentrate, to increase your intake of inositol and choline, and, with some formulae, to provide some of the B vitamins in which your multiple may be lacking or inadequately provided. You are using a separate Vitamin E supplement, in the form of mixed tocopherols, and separate Vitamin B_6.

Lecithin has been mentioned previously, as an aid to fat metabolism, in the control of blood cholesterol, as a means of improving the utilization of fat-soluble vitamins, and for its usefulness in normalizing the redistribution of fat when you are losing weight—a function which it shares with vitamins E and B_6. You can take six 19-grain (1,200 milligram) capsules of lecithin daily, or, if you prefer, use a tablespoonful of the lecithin crystals, which can be added to tomato juice, cereal, applesauce, or similar suitable vehicles. Though the scientific reports don't mention it, lecithin often has an effect similar to that of inositol: quieting. One subject, in an experiment in which we produced redistribution of body fat toward the normal *without* weight loss, remarked that lecithin for her was a "blanket of peace." Please don't take it personally, but I don't trust your food selections prior to encountering me, and for that reason I prefer to prod you into adding lecithin to your list of supplements. I have long been convinced that this compound has a beneficial effect on liver function, which may not only explain its usefulness in the treatment of atherosclerosis (hardening of the arteries) but also fits it neatly into the nutritional program of a book aimed at more efficient control of estrogen metabolism.

The Vitamin C level of the multiple formula—250 milligrams—has been described as minimal. It is far more than is needed to avoid scurvy, but our goal is beyond that, and beyond the prevention of colds. If you will reread the discussion of the Pauling-Cameron research with Vitamin C in terminal cancer, in Chapter 5, you will realize that an optimal intake of this nutrient may be critical in preventing or mitigating malignancies. Dr. Pauling, with whom I have discussed many aspects of his pioneering research, is identified in the public's mind as an advocate of astronomical doses of the vitamin, and does in fact recommend very high doses in the treatment of certain disorders. Overlooked is his estimate of the levels needed to maintain superior health. He states it as a range, from 250 to 2,500 milligrams daily, the latter being, if you will recall, the amount man would be synthesizing daily if evolutionary changes had not deprived him of the ability. That is why I described the 250 milligrams in the multiple vitamin formula as minimal. The ideal intake for an individual—with whom I cannot deal, for a book by definition can't escape generalizations—must be determined by the person. A good index might be subjective criteria, like the feeling of well-being, and objective criteria, like the incidence of colds—their frequency, severity, and duration—for Vitamin C certainly raises resistance to them. Most people will find a level of intake of the vitamin which will yield such dividends. One starts with the amount in the multiple formula, raising it by 100 or 200 milligrams monthly until the optimal amount is found. This will, of course, require adding tablets of ascorbic acid to the list of supplements. If the acidity of ascorbic acid is disturbing—which it is to some people tending toward hyperacidity—sodium ascorbate can be used. It is the same vitamin with the acidity neutralized, though this form can't be used by those on a low-salt diet.

If you bruise easily, or if an IUD contraceptive device causes bleeding, in the absence of organic disease, adding bioflavonoids to the intake of Vitamin C may be helpful. The quantities—in milligrams—should match those of the Vitamin C supplement, and there are concentrates which combine these factors, giving you both ascorbic acid and bioflavonoids in the same tablet. Parenthetically, you lose bioflavonoids when you strain your fruit juices, particularly citrus juices. Don't strain them. Better yet, eat the whole fruit.

What with the arbitrariness of choices of nutrients in formulas for supplements, it is possible you will have difficulty in finding a multiple or a Vitamin B Complex concentrate which offers selenium, or one which offers enough. To cover that contingency, let me note that organically bound selenium, which is the form in which this nutrient should be used, is now available. Because of its interaction with Vitamin E, there are supplements which combine selenium with that vitamin, though the samples I have examined offered only alpha tocopherol, rather than the mixed tocopherols. Potencies begin at about 25 micrograms (1/1,000 of a milligram) daily. Between 25 and 50 micrograms would be a desirable supplementary level.

It is passing strange that a public which confidently swallows sugar—a dangerous food—by the ton will hesitate in taking vitamin and mineral supplements which present no dangers. Part of this apprehension has deliberately been fanned by industries that make junk foods, which will be the first to be discarded if the public experiences the benefits of good nutrition. Part originates with baseless warnings by government agencies, the executives of which came from the junk food industry and will return to it, in the revolving-door tradition. A good example is the purported toxicity of Vitamin A in doses larger than 10,000 units daily. I bring this up because it is necessary to give you several cautions which do not arise from characteristics of vitamin supplements, but from the quirks of the biochemistries of some of those who may take them.

1. The recommendations in this book are intended for "normal" women. (I said they could be cured, remember?) They are not intended for self-treatment of disease. If you have cystic mastitis or uterine fibroid tumors or endometriosis, you are not average, and the diet and supplements should not be used without your physician's knowledge. This is not based on adverse reactions—I've never seen any, save for allergic responses. It simply reflects my belief that the physician who realizes what dividends can accrue from control of estrogen activity by food will be encouraged to apply that to other women. It is also based on the fact that

self-medication for any disorder is unwise, if only because you may not realize that other problems are present, and being neglected.

2. If you're hypertensive, Vitamin E must be used under medical supervision. There are rare individuals with hypertension whose blood pressure rises when the vitamin is first taken. This doesn't preclude their using it, but requires initial small doses, gradually rising, with the pressure checked regularly. The effect isn't seen in people whose blood pressure is normal.

3. If your blood uric acid is elevated, which might mean a tendency toward gout, high doses of Vitamin C—higher than the supplementary level suggested in this book—may elevate the uric acid level. The effect is very rare, and again, doesn't occur in average persons. It may be cancelled by supplements of folic acid in small amounts. The amount of folic acid provided by the recommended menus and supplements should cancel this effect, since folic acid helps to block abnormal synthesis of uric acid.

4. Allergic reactions to vitamins or minerals can occur, as they occur to brewer's yeast or to any other food. Such reactions are difficult to trace, for one can be sensitive to the excipient used in a tablet, rather than to the vitamins it contains; or to a remaining trace of a solvent used in concentrating the nutrients. Rereading Chapter 7 may be useful for readers with allergies.

We have already discussed the special-purpose foods which are used as supplements—brewer's yeast and desiccated liver. Recently, manufacturers have created tablets combining these fine foods, which makes for convenience. Whether you use them thus or take them separately, be sure to take enough, as directed in Chapter 6. They are a great lift toward optimal nutrition, and specifically helpful to liver function. If allergy or intolerance preclude using them, you may still be able to employ wheat germ, rice polishings, and bran in your cereals and recipes, both baked and cooked. If those aren't tolerated, faithful following of the food framework, plus the use of the multiple vitamin–mineral and other supplements will still help you toward the excellent nutrition needed for management of estrogen activity. Not to shut out those who have multiple allergies and aren't able to use *any* of the supplements or special purpose foods: benefits can be had from the food framework alone. Optimal intake of the critical nutrients won't be achieved, which forecloses optimal response, and the process will take years, rather than months—but I need not tell you that it's still worth the effort. A medical nutritionist can often help such violently allergic people to tolerate the allergens to which they react.

The most important warning of all: dividends from good nutrition take time. Many of them accrue reasonably quickly—heightened well-being, increased resistance to fatigue, more restful sleeping, reduced irritability and nervousness, lessened anxiety, clearer thinking. As against these subjective reactions, there are some which are objective: fewer colds, quicker response to medication when sick, and faster convalescence. But with the goal of this book, you have the potential for a reasonably fast and very objective measure of your response to improved nutrition. It should take no more than six months, and it often takes less. For a small percentage of women, there is a paradoxical fast reaction: the first month, their premenstrual symptoms and menstrual discomforts *increase*, and improve slowly thereafter. This reflects in such women a short rise in estrogen output, which has no significance except for its temporary action on the first menstruation following the change in the diet. After this, the liver "catches up," and normalizes estrogen activity, exactly as it did in the prisoners of war. For the very large majority of women, premenstrual symptoms fade gradually, without the paradoxical reaction, diminishing over a few months until the period comes literally without warning, the intensity of the hemorrhaging reduces, and the duration drops from five days to three. For some six women in ten, on the basis of my twenty-five years of observation, by six months the Curse becomes what it should be—a quiet reminder from nature that you chose, that month, not to become pregnant.

Firm prophecies are more difficult to make for women with cystic mastitis, uterine fibroid tumors, and endometriosis. I've already indicated that cystic mastitis is more likely to respond than the other disorders, though they, too, will at least occasionally show improvement. The time-span is about the same—six months, with no paradoxical worsening of the symptoms at any time. Some responses are so gradual that time must pass before you fully realize that there has been a significant improvement. In some women with cystic mastitis, improvement has been dramatic and fast.

For some women, the arrow of good nutrition misses its specific target. It may be that faulty liver control of estrogen isn't responsible for their troubles. But I don't count these as total failures, for these women still reap dividends from better nutrition. Their hair, nails, and complexions improve. Their subjective feeling of well-being is heightened. Often personalities alter for the better. If that thought startles you, you should remember that we are what we eat—and we think with it as well.*

Beyond all these goals beckons that great one which necessitated the writing of this book—that of achieving the negative dividend of what doesn't happen. I am hopeful that you will strive for that. It has been said that the warnings of wisdom are not heard. If heard, they are not believed. If believed, they are not thought to apply to the believer. But, as John Donne reminded us, you cannot ask for whom the bell tolls. It tolls for you.

* *PsychoNutrition*, also published by Grosset & Dunlap, is a text I devoted to the role of nutrition in mental and nervous disorders, ranging from simple neurosis to schizophrenia, autism, depression, hyperactivity, and other disturbances which are not always "all in your mind."

Appendix

I promised you a delightful recipe for an improved white bread. Here it is:

DR. CLIVE MCKAY'S TRIPLE-RICH CORNELL BREAD

This is a high-protein, high-vitamin, high-mineral bread, restoring many of the nutritional values depleted in the milling of white flour, and vastly improving on ordinary white bread. Moreover, it is perfectly acceptable to the majority of white-bread devotees, many of whom will not accept whole-wheat bread. The Cornell mix itself is simple: in an 8-oz. measuring cup, put in 1 Tbs. soy flour, 1 tsp. wheat germ, and 1 Tbs. nonfat dry milk powder. Now fill the cup with white flour, preferably unbleached. Thoroughly stirred, this is now used to make a bread which closely resembles ordinary white bread in appearance, but is flavorful and nutritious. It is a perfect way to outflank the family who as yet will not accept whole grains, though its lack of bran keeps it from being a complete substitute for whole wheat. (The bran has unique values in the human diet, but you can work it in in other ways—bran muffins, for instance.) To make the bread, use about 6 cups of well-mixed and sifted Cornell mix. Have on hand:

2 Tbs. vegetable oil (without additives)
1 Tbs. sea salt
2 Tbs. dry yeast (granule form—available at health food stores)
2 Tbs. honey
3 cups warm water

Soften 2 Tbs. of the yeast in 3 cups of water. Add the honey. Mix the sea salt with 3 cups of the Cornell mix. When the yeast-honey-water mixture bubbles, gradually add to it the 3 cups of Cornell mix, beating it by hand about 70 or 80 times. You can use an electric mixer, but hand-beaten, it somehow turns out better for me. Now add the 2 Tbs. of oil, and enough of the remaining Cornell mix to form it into a dough which is moderately stiff. Knead this on a flour board until its texture is smooth and elastic. Then shape it into a ball, place it in a bowl greased with a little oil, and oil the top of the ball.

You are now ready to let it rise: just cover it and put it in a warm place—which doesn't mean oven heat—until it rises to about double the original size. That should take about 45 minutes.

Now use your fist to deflate the ball, fold the edges in, and turn it upside down, letting it rise again for another 20 minutes. Now turn the dough out on the board (which should still be floured). Split the dough into 3 approximately equal parts, and fold each one inward until it is a smooth and tight ball. (One of these can be used to make rolls, if you wish, as a pleasant change of pace for breakfast.) Cover these with a cloth, and wait 10 minutes. You are now ready to shape each of the 3 into loaves, and put them in oiled bread pans.

In about 45 minutes, the loaves should double in bulk, and you are now ready for baking, at 325° F. for 45 minutes, or so. (Vague, because ovens differ in characteristics; 50 minutes may be necessary. The appearance of the loaves will tell you, when you have gained a little experience.)

As another example of the palatability of foods which are good nutrition, try the following recipe, contributed to the cause by Mrs. Fredericks. Note the small amount of sugar, in contrast to the average cookie recipe. I hope I've well and truly made my point: eating nutrition that protects you doesn't mean meals that you endure for the sake of the cause.

BETTY'S COOKIES

1 cup butter or margarine
3 Tbs. sugar
1 egg, or 2 yolks
2 tsp. baking powder
1 tsp. vanilla
¼ cup soybean flour
2 cups unbleached flour
½ Tbs. wheat germ
3 Tbs. skim-milk solids

Cream butter and sugar. Add egg or yolks and blend well; then add remaining ingredients one by one, mixing thoroughly. Drop by the teaspoonful onto greased baking sheets, or put through a cookie press. Bake at 375° for 15 minutes. *Makes about 4 dozen.*

Note: This recipe is a starting point. The content of soy flour, wheat germ, and skim-milk solids can be raised to reach ultimately a level equivalent to the protein value of meat. Try the recipe in its present form. Next time, raise one of the special ingredients a little. You will discover the level of soybean flour, wheat germ, and skim-milk solids below which you must stay if the cookies are to be pleasing to your family. Even as given above, the recipe is commendably nutritious.

Bibliography

The following citations from the literature in nutrition, medicine, and endocrinology will give you a perspective on the scientific background for this book.

Ablin, Richard J. "Diethylstilbestrol Exposure and Lymphocytic Impairment." *Journal of the American Medical Association (JAMA)*, vol. 229, no. 14, (September 30, 1974), p. 1863.

"Antiestrogens in the Treatment of Cancer." Editorial in *Annals of Internal Medicine*, vol. 84, no. 6, (June 1976), p. 751.

Arehart-Treichel, Joan. "Breast Cancer Update." *Science News*, (February 5, 1977), p. 90.

Arguelles, A. E. "Endocrine Profiles and Breast Cancer." *Lancet*, (January 27, 1973), p. 165.

Ayerst Laboratories, New York. Statement regarding the article "Menopausal Estrogen and Breast Cancer" in the August 19, 1976, issue of the *New England Journal of Medicine*.

Ayre, J. E., and Bauld, W. A. G. *Science*, vol. 103, (1946), p. 441.

Biskind, Morton S. "Nutritional Therapy of Endocrine Disturbances." In *Vitamins and Hormones*, vol. IV, New York: Academic Press, (1946), pp. 147–180.

Blank, Kirby J., et al. "Estrogen Binding in Breast Cancer." *New England Journal of Medicine,* (April 18, 1974), p. 914.

"Breast Cancer and Chemotherapy." *Science,* vol. 192, (June 11, 1976), p. 1062.

"Breast Cancer Research: Problems and Progress." *Science,* vol. 184, (June 14, 1974), p. 1162.

"Breast Cancer Revisited." Editorial in *JAMA,* vol. 232, no. 7, (May 19, 1975).

"Breast Cancer: Second Thoughts about Routine Mammography." *Science,* vol. 193, (August 13, 1976), p. 555.

"Cancer Risk and Estrogen Use in the Menopause." Editorial in *New England Journal of Medicine,* vol. 293, no. 23, (December 4, 1975), p. 1199.

Chopra, I. J., et al. "Estrogen-Androgen Imbalance in Hepatic Cirrhosis: Studies in 13 Male Patients." *JAMA,* vol. 226, no. 5, (October 29, 1973), p. 580.

Cole, Philip, et al. "Estrogen Profiles of Parous and Nulliparous Women." *Lancet,* (September 18, 1976), p. 596.

"The Controversy Over 'The Pill.' " *Executive Health,* vol. XIII, no. 1, (October 1976).

"Dangers in Eternal Youth." *Lancet,* (December 6, 1975), p. 1135.

Deanesley, Margaret. "Breast Prostheses." *JAMA,* vol. 236, no. 5, (August 2, 1976), p. 499.

Dickinson, Louis E., et al. "Profiles of Oriental and Caucasian Women in Hawaii." *New England Journal of Medicine,* vol. 291, no. 23, (December 5, 1973), p. 1211.

"Diethylstilbestrol." *Medical World News,* (August 23, 1976), p. 44.

Edmondson, Hugh H., et al. "Liver Cell Adenomas Associated with Use of Oral Contraceptives." *New England Journal of Medicine,* (February 26, 1976), p. 470.

"Endocrine Profiles and Breast Cancer." *Lancet,* (March 10, 1973), p. 546.

Enstrom, James E., and Austin, Donald F. "Interpreting Cancer Survival Rates." *Science,* vol. 195, (March 4, 1977), p. 847.

Epstein, Samuel S. "The Political and Economic Basis of Cancer." *Technology Review*, (July–August 1976), p. 35.

"Estriol and Prevention of Breast Cancer." *Lancet*, (March 10, 1973), p. 546.

"Estrogen-Binding Protein in Blood to Predict Response of Breast Cancer to Hormone Manipulation." *Lancet*, (July 17, 1976), p. 145.

"Estrogens and the Menopause." *JAMA*, vol. 227, no. 3, (January 21, 1974), p. 318.

"Estrogen Drugs: Do They Increase the Risk of Cancer?" *Science*, vol. 191, (February 27, 1976), p. 838.

"Estrogen Profiles of Parous and Nulliparous Women." *JAMA*, vol. 236, no. 24, (December 13, 1976), p. 2811.

Everson, Richard B., et al. "Familial Male Breast Cancer." *Lancet*, (January 3, 1976), p. 9.

"Exposure in Utero to Diethylstilbestrol and Related Synthetic Hormones." *JAMA*, vol. 236, no. 10, (September 6, 1976), p. 1109.

Fisher, Richard I., et al. "Estrogen Receptors in Human Malignant Melanoma." *Lancet*, (August 14, 1976), p. 337.

Fredericks, Carlton. "Nutritional Management of Estrogen-Dependent Disorders." *Journal: International Academy of Metabology*, vol. IV, no. I, (1972), p. 17.

Goodman, Robin Reba. *Gynecology or Genocide?* Santa Ana, California: Feminist Women's Center, 1974.

Hayden, S. *The Role of Fats in Human Nutrition*. New York: Academic Press, 1975, p. 96. See Appendix: "Possible Side Effects of Dietary Fats."

Henderson, Brian E., et al. "Elevated Serum Levels of Estrogen and Prolactin in Daughters of Patients with Breast Cancer." *New England Journal of Medicine*, vol. 293, no. 16, (October 16, 1975), p. 790.

"Higher Cancer 'Cure.' " *JAMA*, vol. 222, no. 4, (October 23, 1972), p. 418.

Hoover, Robert, et al. "Cancer of the Uterine Corpus after Hormonal Treatment for Breast Cancer." *Lancet*, (April 24, 1976), p. 885.

Hoover, Robert, et al. "Menopausal Estrogens and Breast Cancer." *New England Journal of Medicine*, vol. 295, no. 8, (August 19, 1976).

"Hot Flushes and Estrogen Therapy." *Lancet*, (July 17, 1976), p. 152.

"Hot Flushes and Estrogen Therapy." *Lancet*, (August 14, 1976), p. 364.

Kapdi, C. C., and Wolfe, John N. "Breast Cancer: Relationship to Thyroid Supplements for Hypothyroidism." *JAMA*, vol. 236, no. 10, (September 6, 1976), p. 1124.

Kaufman, Raymond, et al. "Severe Atypical Endometrial Changes and Sequential Contraceptive Use." *JAMA*, vol. 236, no. 8, (August 23, 1976), p. 923.

Lemon, Henry M. "Mammary Carcinogenesis." *New England Journal of Medicine*, (May 1, 1975), p. 974.

Lemon, Henry M., et al. "Reduced Estriol Excretion in Patients with Breast Cancer prior to Endocrine Therapy." *JAMA*, vol. 196, no. 13, (June 27, 1966), p. 112.

Levene, Arnold. "Chronic Mastitis and Carcinoma of the Breast." *Lancet*, (August 28, 1976), p. 475.

Lippman, M. "A Demonstration of Androgen and Estrogen Receptors in a Human Breast Cancer Using a New Protamine Sulfate Assay." *JAMA*, vol. 236, no. 23, (December 6, 1976), p. 2692.

"Liver Cell Neoplasms and Oral Contraceptives." *Lancet*, (January 12, 1974), p. 64.

"Mammography: Benefits vs. Risks." *Science News*, vol. 110, (July 31, 1976), p. 70.

Marshall, Byrne R. "Post-Menopausal Vaginal Bleeding During Estrogen Therapy." *JAMA*, vol. 227, no. 1, (January 7, 1974) (Letters). p. 76–77.

Mecklenburg, R. S., and Lipsett, M. B. "Disappearance of Metastatic Breast Cancer after Oophorectomy." *New England Journal of Medicine*, vol. 289, no. 16, (October 18, 1973), p. 845.

Miller, W. R., and Forrest, A. P. M. "Estradiol Synthesis by a Human Breast Carcinoma." *Lancet*, (October 12, 1974), p. 866.

Monson, Richard R., et al. "Chronic Mastitis and Carcinoma of the Breast." *Lancet*, (July 31, 1976), p. 224.

"More Critics Raise Voices Against Estrogen Therapy." *JAMA*, vol. 235, no. 8, (February 23, 1976), p. 787.

"More Studies Suggest Estrogen–Cancer Link." *Medical World News*, (June 28, 1976), p. 21.

"New Risk Factor Found for Breast Cancer." *JAMA*, vol. 222, no. 12, (December 18, 1972), p. 1483.

Nigro, Dennis M., and Organ, Claude H., Jr. "Fibroadenoma of the Female Breast." *Postgraduate Medicine*, vol. 59, no. 5 (May 1976), p. 113.

"Nine out of Ten 'DES Babies' Have Vaginal Adenosis." *Medical World News*, (November 9, 1973), p. 17.

"Our Bodies' Own Cancer Cures." *Modern Maturity*, (December–January, 1976–77), p. 64.

"Prophylactic Treatment Held Possible with Breast Cancer." *JAMA*, vol. 192, no. 6, (May 10, 1965), p. 29.

Proudfit, Carol M. "Estrogens and Menopause." *JAMA*, vol. 236, no. 8, (August 23, 1976), p. 939.

"Receptors: Key to Cancer Hormone Use." *Medical World News*, (December 13, 1976), p. 27.

Sahadevan, V., et al. "Estrogen and Estrogen Receptors of Breast Cancer." *Journal of Surgical Oncology*, vol. 7, no. 6, (1975), p. 467.

Sallan, Stephan, et al. "Antiemetic Effect of Delta Nine Tetrahydrocannabinol in Patients Receiving Cancer Chemotherapy." *New England Journal of Medicine*, (October 16, 1975), p. 795.

Sartwell, Philip E., et al. "Epidemiology of Benign Breast Lesions: Lack of Association with Oral Contraceptive Use." *New England Journal of Medicine*, vol. 288, no. 11, p. 55.

"Selenium and Heart Disease." *JAMA*, vol. 235, no. 22, (May 31, 1976), p. 2387.

"Selenium, the Mineral that May Boost Cancer Resistance." *Prevention*, (August 1976), p. 82.

Shamberger, Raymond J. "GI Tract Cancer Linked to Carcinogen in Beef, Poultry, Pork." *Journal of the National Cancer Institute*, (December 1974).

Skinner, Karen Joy. "Work Clarifies Mechanism of Hormone Action." *Chemical and Engineering News*, (January 31, 1977), p. 22.

Small, Donald M. "Hormone Use to Change Normal Physiology—Is the Risk Worth It?" *New England Journal of Medicine*, (January 22, 1976), p. 219.

Stadel, Bruce V. "Dietary Iodine and Risk of Breast, Endometrial, and Ovarian Cancer." *Lancet*, (April 24, 1976), p. 890.

Stern, Michael P., et al. "Cardiovascular Risk and Use of Estrogens or Estrogen-Progestagen Combinations." *JAMA*, vol. 235, no. 8, (February 23, 1976), p. 811.

Stolley, P.D., et al. "Low Estrogen Oral Contraceptives." *JAMA*, vol. 234, no. 12, (December 22, 1975), p. 1278.

Thalassinos, N. C., et al. "Liver-Cell Carcinoma After Long-Term Estrogenlike Drugs." *Lancet*, (February 16, 1974), p. 270.

"Thyroid Supplements and Breast Cancer." *JAMA*, vol. 236, no. 24, (December 13, 1976), p. 2743.

"Vaginal Adenocarcinomas and Maternal Estrogen Ingestion." *Lancet*, (February 16, 1974), p. 250.

Warburg, Otto. Revised Lecture at the Meeting of Nobel Laureates on June 30, 1966. Trans. by Dean Burke. Wurzburg, Germany: Konrad Triltsch, 1969.

Ward, H. W. C. "To Counter Breast Cancer—An Oral Agent." *British Medical Journal*, vol. 1, (1973), p. 13.

Ziel, J. K., and Finkle, W. D. "Association of Estrone with Development of Endometrial Carcinoma." *American Journal of Obstetrics and Gynecology*, vol. 124, (April 1, 1976), p. 735.

Index